I0475917

Dialogue & Initiative

2013 Edition

After the 2012 Election: Strategy and Organizing against Racism and the Right

Published by the
Committees of Correspondence Education Fund

Changemaker Publications

Dialogue & Initiative is a discussion journal published by the Committees of Correspondence Education Find, Inc.,

PO Box 437, New York, NY 10018-0008.

(212) 868-3773; Fax: (212) 868-3334

Email: national@cc-ds.org
Web: www.cc-ds.org

Editor: Harry Targ

Editorial Committee: Carl Bloice, Todd Freeberg, Pat Fry, Michael Kaufman,Ted Pearson, Ted Reich, Meta Van Sickle

Layout and design for this issue: Carl Davidson,

Manuscripts not exceeding 5000 words are invited. Send text via email; hard copy can be mailed or faxed. Manuscripts will be returned if a acompanied by postage-paid, self-addressed packaging.

ISBN# 978-1-304-03970-5

http://www.lulu.com/spotlight/changemaker

Table of Contents

Online University of the Left

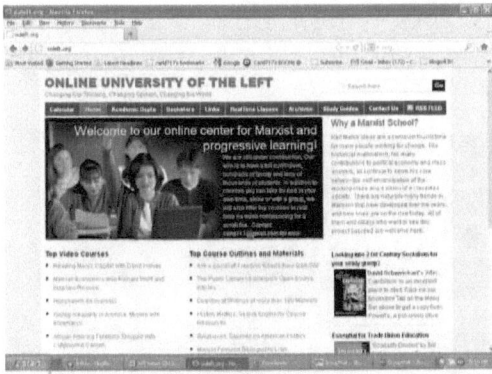

Study!
Teach!
Organize!

We are a free and open university with all the diverse views on the left. We are inspired by Karl Marx, whose ideas are a common touchstone for many people working for change. His historical materialism, his many contributions to political economy and class analysis, all continue to serve our core values--the self-emancipation of the working class and a vision of a classless society. There are naturally many trends in Marxism that have developed over the years, and new ones are on the rise today. All of them, and other radicals and progressives who want to see this project succeed, are welcome here.

- Free political and cultural programming with hundreds of video classes

- Ideal for book store programs, book promotions & study groups

- Faculty: get 'double duty' out of your online materials by placing them here as well

- Course outlines & in-depth text archives; use for teach-ins. Just get a projector and a screen!

- Coming soon! Interactive classes in real time for a small fee.

- Speakers also available

- Your input & feedback is welcome! Use our Facebook page, too!

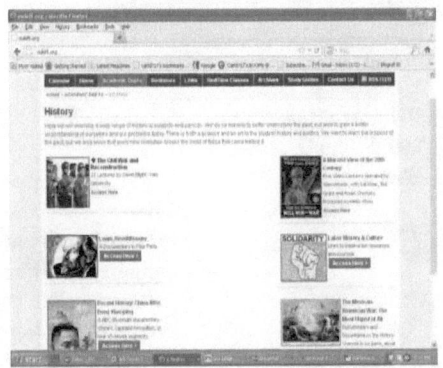

http://ouleft.org

A Left Unity Project of the Committees of Correspondence for Democracy and Socialism
Http://cc-ds.org To get involved, contact: Carl Davidson at carld717@gmail.com

Take a Free Subscription to Our Weekly E-Newsletter...

Easy to sign on and to unsubscribe as well. Go to http://tinyurl. com.ccdslinks, pick a back issue, and click the button in the left column. Arrives every Friday AM

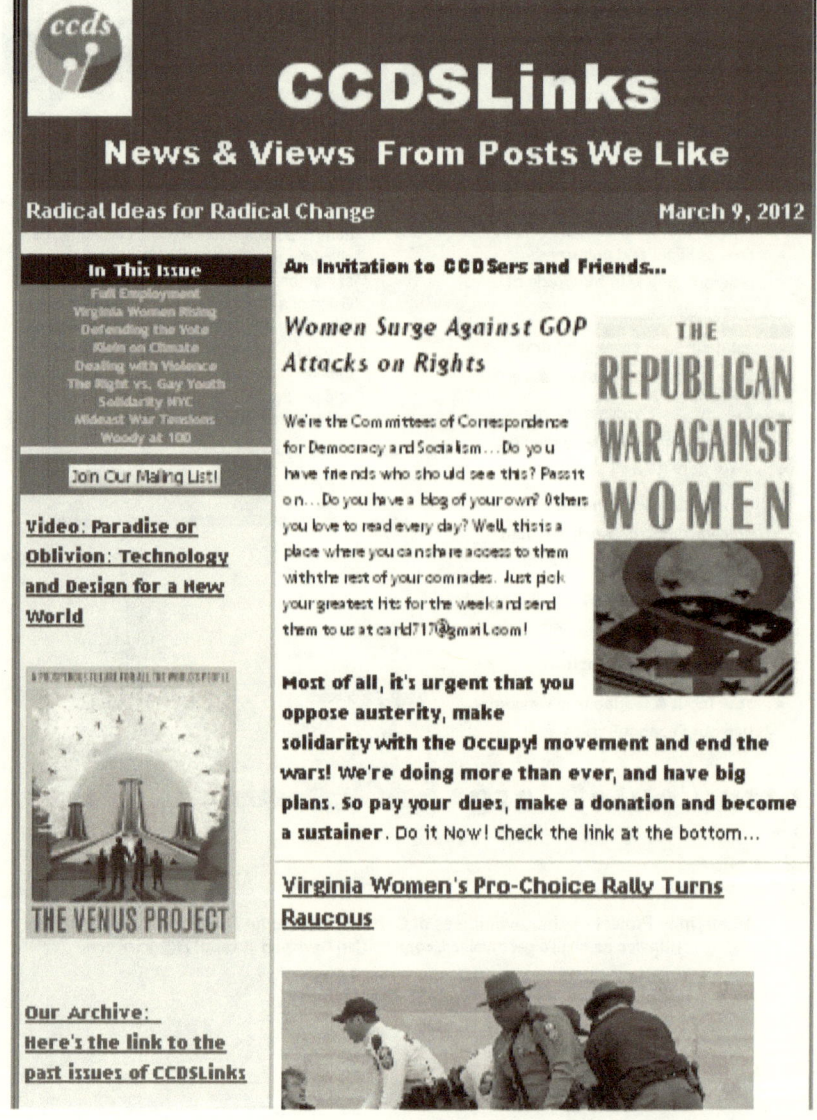

How the Left Can Become a True Political Force to Be Reckoned With after the 2012 Election

By Bill Fletcher & Carl Davidson
Alternet.org

Nov 13, 2012 - The 2012 elections may prove to have been a watershed in several different respects. Despite the efforts by the political Right to suppress the Democratic electorate, something very strange happened: voters, angered by the attacks on their rights, turned out in even greater force in favor of Democratic candidates. The deeper phenomenon is that the changing demographics of the USA also became more evident—45% of Obama voters were people of color, and young voters turned out in large numbers in key counties.

Unfortunately for the political Left, these events unfolded with the Left having limited visibility and a limited impact—except indirectly through certain mass organizations—on the outcome.

The setting

On one level it is easy to understand why many Republicans found it difficult to believe that Mitt Romney did not win the election. First, the US remains in the grip of an economic crisis with an official unemployment rate of 7.9%. In some communities, the unemployment is closer to 20%. While the Obama administration had taken certain steps to address the economic crisis, the steps have been insufficient in light of the global nature of the crisis. The steps were also limited by the political orientation of the Obama administration, i.e., corporate liberal, and the general support by many in the administration for neo-liberal economics.

The second factor that made the election a "nail biter" was the amount of money poured into this contest. Approximately $6 billion was spent in the entire election. In the Presidential race it was more than $2 billion raised and spent, but this does not include independent expenditures. In either case, this was the first post-Citizen United Presidential campaign, meaning that money was flowing into this election like a flood after a dam bursts. Republican so-called Super Political Action Committees (Super PACs) went all out to defeat President Obama.

Third, the Republicans engaged in a process of what came to be known as "voter suppression" activity. Particularly in the aftermath of the 2010 midterm elections, the Republicans created a false crisis of alleged voter fraud as a justification for various draconian steps aimed at allegedly cleansing the election process of illegitimate voters. Despite the fact that the Republicans could not substantiate their claims that voter fraud was a problem on any scale, let alone a significant problem, they were able to build up a clamor for restrictive changes in the process, thereby permitting the introduction of various laws to make it more difficult for voters to cast their ballots. This included photographic voter identification, more difficult processes for voter registration, and the shortening of early voting. Though many of these steps were overturned through the intervention of courts, they were aimed at causing a chilling impact on the voters, specifically, the Democratic electorate.[1]

So, what happened?

Prior to the election, we argued that what was at stake in the 2012 elections was actually the changing demographics of the USA (along with a referendum on the role of government in the economy). What transpired in the elections was very much about demographics.

The percentage of white voters dropped from 74% to 72% between 2008 and 2012. Romney received 59% of the white vote.

Yet something else happened and it took many people by surprise. Despite the intimidation caused by the voter suppression statutes—and the threatened actions by right-wing groups—African Americans, Latinos and Asians turned out in significant numbers, voting overwhelmingly for the Democrats.[2] 93% of African Americans went with Obama, as did 71% of Latinos (which represented an increase over 2008) and, despite the fact that Asians are only 2-3% of the electorate, they went 73% in favor of Obama (which was a jump from 62% in 2008). The youth vote, by the way, increased to 19% of the electorate, over 18% in 2008, and went overwhelmingly for Obama. Labor union members went for Obama at a rate of 65%, and unions themselves played a major role in many key states in terms of voter mobilization. By the strategic mobilization of these voters in a well-organized "ground game," Obama won 332 Electoral College votes compared with Romney's 206. Obama's popular vote total was also 2.6% head of Romney.

The Romney/Ryan camp was entirely unprepared for this. While it is the case that the popular vote total was not overwhelming for Obama, there was nothing particularly unusual in US history for such a result. The bottom line is that Obama clearly won both the Electoral College vote and the popular vote and, as such, can claim a mandate for his next steps.
It is important that one understands that the African American/Latino/Asian turnout, along with the long-lines waiting to vote (including in the days of early voting) represented an audacious defiance of the forces that sought to suppress the vote. This audaciousness also represented a response to the increasingly racist attacks on Obama, attacks that were taken very personally by people of color generally and African Americans in particular.[3]

What was equally interesting about the November 6th elections were those in the House of Representatives and the Senate. Contrary to many expectations, the Democrats not only held onto the Senate, but slightly increased their margin of control. Within that expansion was the election of Elizabeth Warren from Massachusetts to the seat once occupied by the late Teddy Kennedy. Warren, who gained a strong reputation in the fight to control Wall Street, promised actions on behalf of working people. Independent Senator Bernie Sanders, a socialist in Vermont, also decisively won reelection.

In the House of Representatives, Democrats increased their totals, but Republicans still dominate. This is mainly the result of the gerrymandering carried out by Republican state legislators during redistricting. The legacy of this gerrymandering may last at least a decade, part of the fallout which resulted from lower voter turnout combined with the Republican mobilization in the 2010 midterm elections.

Of particular note in the elections was the increased presence of women, especially progressive women, being elected to office, including the first openly gay Senator (from Wisconsin, Tammy Baldwin). The state of New Hampshire now has women in all of the top governing positions.

Additionally several progressive ballot initiatives passed in various states, including on same-sex marriage and the decriminalization of marijuana. An interesting initiative in the state of Michigan to alter the state constitution in order to protect the right of workers to collective bargaining was defeated after a major and concerted attack by pro-employer groups.

What to make of the elections?

We return to our earlier conclusion, i.e., that what was at stake in 2012 was not Obama's record but instead 2012 was a referendum over demographics and the role of government with the far right. Some on the Left found this assertion worthy of ridicule rather than introspection, and dismissed it, claiming that of course Obama's record was central to the debate.

The results of the election conform much more to our conclusions. The vote for Obama, particularly by people of color, could not possibly have been the result of the conclusion that Obama's record made him the great leader. Certainly his record was better than the interpretation projected by Romney/Ryan, but it was also the case that Obama's record was complicated if not problematic. After all, we had witnessed an economic stimulus that, while significant by historical standards, was insufficient to the task; a healthcare reform package that, while bringing healthcare to millions, was based on a corporate model first elaborated by Mitt Romney when he was Governor of Massachusetts; a failure to close Guantanamo; the continuation and escalation of the Afghanistan/ Pakistan war, including the usage of drone strikes; and the failure to adopt a clear policy to address systemic racial injustice in the USA. While there were a number of reforms that were introduced that were of significance, this was all far less than most of Obama's supporters had hoped would be introduced.

So, what then could one say motivated the vote? We return to demographics and the role of government. Obama's very existence represents the problematic future for the political Right; it's not that he's an individual whose birthplace is alleged by them to not be in the USA. This insane propaganda from the Birther movement is designed to distort the point entirely. The Birthers[4] and their off-spring hate Obama not because of where he was born but because he was born here. His very existence illustrates the changing demographics of the USA and its move away from being a "white republic" governed by a broad "white" front. Instead, we are moving more towards something else, toward a more openly multi-ethnic/multi-racial society, if not politically then at least numerically.

The election thus represented a repudiation of the right-wing irrationalists seeking to turn the clock back and not just on race, but gender and class as well. In this sense it was not so much about what Obama had accomplished as it was about what sort of society 61 million people did not want. That retrograde society, which was rejected, was a neo-apartheid order of domination that condemned at least 47% of the population (according to Romney's calculations) to marginalization, and condemned at least 90% of society to continued economic distress and submission. Romney was proposing to reduce the role of government even further, at least when it came to supporting something approaching a social safety net. 61 million people recognized the barbarism contained in his message and program, and responded accordingly.

In sum, the November 6th elections were not a referendum challenging Obama's course from the Left, but rather rejecting a challenge from the Right, since there was no viable Left alternative. At the same time there was an additional interesting feature of the elections as identified in various opinion polls: Democratic voters, while not as starry-eyed as many were in 2008, are looking for Obama to fight for them, or at least fight on their behalf. Frustration with Obama's premature compromising in the name of so-called bi-partisanship wins the President few accolades within his base. The electorate is looking for something very different. The Left in the elections: Building mass organizations vs. the mouths that screeched

The Two-and-a-Half Lefts in the US

Contrary to those who suggest that no Left exists in the USA, it is better to understand that there are two and a half Lefts in the USA. There is the organized Left, which takes the forms of very small political organizations, some of them calling themselves political parties, which are anti-capitalist and generally for some sort of socialism. There is also what Chilean Marxist Marta Harnecker would describe as the "social movement Left," which are forces involved in left-leaning mass organizations and non-profits, more often than not single-issue or based within a specific sector. There is finally what we could term the "half" Left, that is, the "Lone Rangers," the rather large number of independent individuals who self-identify as leftists but are unaffiliated with any left-wing project, with the possible exception a job with social impact, such as writers or teachers or health care workers. In each case these individuals and formations are anti-capitalist and seek a social transformation of the USA, but with varying degrees of organization, insurgency and effectiveness.

The US Left has historically had a difficult time addressing electoral politics. There are several reasons--the complications that arise from the undemocratic nature of the US electoral system; the size of the USA; the lack of attention to strategy; and most important, ambivalence when it comes to race.

As a result the Left frequently sways back and forth between what could, perhaps, be described as apocalyptism on the one hand (i.e., waving the red flag so that the masses see us before the whole system collapses and, therefore, they know where to go), to reformist/incrementalism, on the other (i.e., believing that the best that can be done is to submerge into the Democratic Party and help move change until the system reaches a point where quantitative change morphs into qualitative change).

There is currently no significant and unified effort within the Left(s) toward building a self-conscious, broad radical Left project that has the objective of winning power. The bulk of the US Left does not think politically. Rather it engages in ideological or moral struggle and often thinks that ideology or morality is identical to politics. Rather than conceptualizing a protracted struggle for power based on the need to build a majoritarian bloc, too many individuals and organizations on the Left remain trapped in a self-satisfying world of small sects and Facebook tirades rather than the hard work of building the alliances of grassroots groups necessary to win.

The limitations of the Left's approach to the fight for power can be illustrated in any number of places, but, for the moment, let's reflect upon the electoral realm. Consider the following. In 1920 Eugene V. Debs ran, for the fifth time, for the Presidency. Though in jail at the time (as a result of political repression), he received nearly one million votes. In the famous 1948 campaign of Progressive Party candidate Henry Wallace, the candidate received 1,157,328 votes and no Electoral College votes. In the same election, Dixiecrat candidate Strom Thurmond received more popular votes and 39 electoral votes.

Now, in 2012, Green Party candidate Jill Stein received 402,125 votes. This is going the wrong way. But it reflects, more than anything, not the character of Stein or her supporters but the approach toward electoral politics taken by the Green Party and many of their followers.

From Protest Mode to Power-Bloc Mode

Independent presidential candidacies in the modern era reflect what can be described as a flag-waving/protest mode rather than a struggle for power/bloc-building mode. In other words, they aim to express both outrage and reasoned critique at the system and frustration with the toxicity of democratic capitalism. They have no hope of gaining power either because they do not believe in struggling to gain power or because they believe that power is gained when the ship sinks and we, on the Left, are positioned in the proper lifeboats prepared to save the mass of distressed passengers.

This is only on the electoral side. The various small organizations of the organized Left which do not engage in electoral politics in their own names seem relatively content being small and of little consequence. In the absence of an effort at building a majoritarian bloc they can remain comfortable in their particular niche(s) and not feel the cold winds that often accompany entering into unexplored demographic or geographic territories. They remind us of the old Clifford Odet's play, Waiting for Lefty.

At the same time, over the last 5-10 years there has developed a new interest in electoral engagement in the social movement Left. Sprouting up in different parts of the USA have been progressive—rather than ex- plicitly Left—political formations that have either engaged in what has come to be known as "civic engagement" work, i.e., voter registration, education, voting rights, electoral law reform, and/or actual electoral engagement. The strength of this work is that its orientation can be described as left/progressive in that these are mass-based projects at- tempting to reach out to a broad array within our natural base. Organi- zations ranging from Progressive Democrats of America, to the Virginia New Majority and Florida New Majority fall into this camp, though the list is quite a bit longer than just these organizations.

In the lead up to the 2012 elections the Left was badly divided over how to respond. One segment, which we will describe as the "mouths that screeched" were adamant that Obama had betrayed progressives; that he was not progressive; that he represented the empire; and therefore not only should not be supported but that it was ideological treason to suggest any level of support or even just to give him a vote without any implied support.

The vitriolic attacks coming from this sector masked the fact that this segment of the Left is actually becoming irrelevant. They had no visible impact on the elections and their protests were largely ignored. Unfor- tunately, one of the key things that this segment missed was the racial element of the 2012 elections and the need for voters of color, along with a good number of white allies, to push back at the "demographic" attacks that were underway from the political Right. By focusing on all that Obama did incorrectly, this segment of the Left ignored, as well, that the Left and progressives are on the strategic defensive in the USA and that they need alliances that will provide some level of space within which we can operate.

The segment of the Left that actually made a difference was those with- in the organized Left and the social movement Left who engaged their mass organizations and non-profits in electoral activity.[5] Whether it was voter registration; voter education efforts; electoral infrastructure work; or Get Out The Vote efforts, many of these organizations proved themselves to be very effective campaign organizations. They appear to be in the process of laying the groundwork for the sorts of progressive alliance building that will be necessary to respond to the next electoral realignment that hits the USA.

What is missing entirely, however, is a coherent, self-identified Left, taking either the form of a united front, alliance, or political organization that can serve as a pole for independent, radical yet grounded Left politics. The mass base for such an effort exists. The opinion polls that demonstrate that roughly one third of the population are open to directions other than capitalism means that approximately 90 million people are seeking alternatives. Consider that 90 million figure when you review the stats for the Green Party's votes in 2012. The Occupy Movement also evidenced a political fissure that is certain to widen as the class struggle intensifies, though admittedly Occupy did not result in the formation of one or several credible Left organizations (no criticism implied).

The challenge for the Left then becomes two fold. One, there must be a self-identified, self-aware, mass radical Left formation that openly and unapologetically advocates against capitalism and for environmentally friendly socialism. Whether such an organization is called a political party, alliance or some other name is secondary to what it must do and what it must avoid. What it must avoid is the idea that it can or should compete in the electoral realm on the presidential level at this time. That is a no-win scenario. What it can do, however, is to unite and train the existing leaders in mass movements and develop an anti-capitalist program and ultimately an anti-capitalist project. We term this notion of a new, self-conscious and organized Left—inspired by the approach taken by and expression used by Italian Marxist Antonio Gramsci—to be the "Modern Tecumseh."[6] Second, the Left can also help to build a progressive front—perhaps a popular front against finance capital that unites disparate forces—that gains electoral expression in the form of an organization (rather than a third party) that runs candidates within the Democratic Party or, runs them independently if conditions exist (such as in Vermont where the candidacy and leadership of Senator Sanders needs to be supported).

As long as the progressive forces in the USA are on the defensive there will be tactical alliances that take place that are not satisfying but are nevertheless necessary. These should not be treated as matters of principle but rather as expressions of necessity of the moment. Further, we on the Left must pay much greater attention to what is transpiring among the people themselves. The fact that so many on the Left would have focused on Obama's record and virtually ignored the intense racist offensive against Obama (and its broader implications) demonstrated that many of our friends are out of touch with reality.

Reality, however, is a good and necessary starting point if one ever wishes to build a majoritarian bloc and win power. We fully expect to see an intensification of class struggle in the near term. We need to assert a new culture of organizing capable of meeting the demands it will place on us, and now is the time to begin.

[1] The issue of voting rights remains critical since there are cases before the US Supreme Court to challenge critical features of the 1965 Voting Rights Act, features that were part of the Department of Justice's arsenal to overturn certain voter suppression legislation.

[2] It is important to note, however, that voter turnout was down in comparison to 2008 except for nine states. As of this writing it is not clear as to the sources of the decline.

[3] Attacks such as Donald Trump's insulting demand that President Obama turn over his college transcripts. The suggestion of such an action is almost unbelievable. Nothing along those lines would have been tolerated when it came to former President George W. Bush, an individual who was not half the student that was Obama in college.

[4] The right-wing, irrationalist political movement that asserts that Obama was not born in the USA and is, therefore, not the legitimate president of the USA.

[5] To be clear, not all forces in the organized Left or the social movement Left engaged in left/progressive electoral organizing. We are simply noting that there were forces from within these sectors that did, in fact, choose to engage.

[6] Tecumseh: Shawnee leader in the first decade of the 19th century. Recognized that Native Americans would never defeat the USA by fighting as individual tribes or fighting through the creation of a confederation. He was the advocate for a Native American nation-state, i.e., uniting the tribes and fusing their efforts. He was killed in 1813 at the Battle of the Thames in Canada.

Bill Fletcher, Jr. is a racial justice, labor and international writer and activist. He is a Senior Scholar with the Institute for Policy Studies, an editorial board member of BlackCommentator.com, and the co-author of Solidarity Divided. Email: billfletcherjr@gmail.com

Carl Davidson is a writer and public speaker. He is currently co-chair of CCDS, a board member of the US Solidarity Economy Network. His most recent book is 'New Paths to Socialism: Essays on the Mondragon Cooperatives, Workplace Democracy and the Politics of Transition.' Email: carld717@gmail.com.

Time of Day: Three Crises Converging

By Pat Fry,
CCDS National Co-Chair

The time of day is likely the most challenging in history as we are confronted by a convergence of 3 crises: the economy, militarism and war, and the climate. Limited time in this presentation allows only to briefly touch on each.

The Climate

With little media attention in early April a Little Rock, Arkansas suburban neighborhood was flooded with thick, dangerous oil running through its streets and storm sewers on its way to the Arkansas River that flows into the Mississippi. The leak was from an ExxonMobil pipeline the cause of which remains a mystery. The neighborhood did not even know they had pipeline below their land. The area has been under a "no-fly zone" and reporters are barred. This is the same thick oil that will flow through the XL Keystone pipeline if allowed to proceed and run across the country from north to south.

This is the same type of disaster that occurred in 2010 in Kalamazoo, Michigan when an Enbridge owned-and-operated pipeline burst and dumped an unknown amount of tar sands oil into the Kalamazoo River, polluting 40 miles of river and wetlands and then into Lake Michigan. The Kalamazoo River clean-up is now in its third year.

These oil spills should be a "huge and loud wake up call to all of us, especially lawmakers," wrote Stewart Acuff, former organizing director of the AFL-CIO on his blog. "It is the same kind of oil that would flow through the very controversial XL Keystone pipeline. Exxon has done a great job rewarding their friends. So far the members of the Arkansas Congressional delegation who supported the XL Keystone pipeline before this disaster continue to support XL," wrote Acuff.

Exxon Mobil is the world's second largest oil company with annual profits of $41 billion. It is the largest U.S. corporation, and pays no or little US federal taxes over the past 5 years.

War and Militarism

Closely connected to Big Oil and the climate crisis is the military-industrial complex that fuels US- sponsored endless wars and drone attacks. The U.S. military provocations toward North Korea are one of the latest examples. The CCDS Peace and Solidarity committee has issued a statement calling for the US to cease its provocations, hypocrisy and arrogance and urging a negotiated end to the Korean War once and for all. In this, CCDS joins with other peace voices such as the American Friends Service Committee.

On the gun control issue being debated in Congress and the growth of US right wing armed terrorists, Julie Burkhart has become an open target. In early April Burkhart reopened an abortion clinic in Witchita, KS with public threats on her life. This is the same clinic where Dr. George Tiller worked when he was assassinated in his church 4 years ago. This is certainly bravery in the defense of women's reproductive rights. Federal troops should be called in to protect this clinic and arrest the terrorists.

The gun issue has become a rallying cry for the far-right and an opportunity to promote private security and militias. In Nelson, GA the Tea Party-led city council passed an ordinance requiring all residents to have guns and ammunition, evidently part of an effort to privatize local law enforcement and promote vigilantism.

The Economy

Carl Bloice, in his weekly column in the Black Commentator summed up the crisis as "Austerity 2013 – US Style." He described the "double whammy" on the working class: a grim jobs report, on the one hand, and on the other, a grand betrayal by the Obama White House calling for cuts to Social Security and Medicare to appease Wall Street deficit hawks.

We must proclaim loudly and clearly with feet marching on the ground: we need Jobs, Jobs, Jobs – No to Cuts. We have to educate about how the debt accumulated in the first place: two criminal wars against Afghanistan and Iraq, Bush era tax cuts and the bank bails-outs in response to their criminal fraud.

Wall Street's demand for deficit reduction is a cover for austerity in providing socially necessary programs, and the Obama White House is going along with it at the expense of working and retired people, veterans and the disabled, the poor and children.

Economists such as Paul Krugman have long argued that there is no economic growth in cutting deficits. The 2010 paper "Growth in the Time of Debt" by two Harvard economists, Reinhart and Rogoff, has been used to justify austerity here and around the world. Its recent exposure falsely reporting on data should end the argument for austerity. The time to spend on social programs and putting people to work is now, urgently now.

Millions Unemployed

The official March jobs report shows 11.7 million people are out of work. The unemployment rate fell slightly to 7.6% in March but not for good reasons. People are dropping out of the labor force. The labor participation rate of 63.3% is the lowest of the Great Recession. The drop is not due to workers retiring. It's the lack of jobs. African American unemployment continues in the double digits at twice the rate of whites. Quoted in Bloice's Black Commentator article was author Tamara Draut who said "The deep and persistent high levels of joblessness and under-employment among young people without 4-year degrees is a silent crisis facing our nation. And it demands a robust and national response."

She is absolutely right. The jobs crisis, not the deficit, must be our rallying cry. The Congressional Progressive Caucus released its "Back to Work" budget that would put people to work in public works and cut the military budget but it hardly had a hearing in Congress or in the media.

The Sequester caused by Republican intransigence on the budget will result in 140,000 families losing their homes with the loss of Section 8 vouchers, and 750,000 more jobs lost in the public sector, disproportionately affecting African Americans.

I have been spending the last two months in my home state of Michigan where the unemployment rate remains officially at 8.9% and where more than half of the state's 1.5 million Black population has been brought under dictatorial rule. The majority African American cities of Detroit, Flint, Pontiac, Benton Harbor, Highland Park, Ecorse, and Hamtramck have been taken over by an Emergency Financial Manager installed by the Republican Gov. Rick Snyder. The EFM in each of these cities removed legislative power from the Mayor and City Councils.

Using budget shortfalls, real and contrived, Gov. Snyder lays blame on unions and "irresponsible leadership" of elected officials, mostly whom are Black. The EFMs are shredding union contracts, laying off public workers, slashing pensions, and selling off public lands and assets. In Pontiac, one of the states' abandoned auto centers located just north of Detroit, salaries were terminated for the Mayor and City Councilpersons and legislative powers taken away two years ago.

The city workforce was slashed from 1,000 jobs to 60 today. The Pontiac Silverdome, former home to the Detroit Lions which was built with tax-payer money and valued at $22 million, was sold for the bargain-basement price of $535,000. Even the plumbing was worth more. It's been reported that the EFM that sold the stadium tried to go into business with the person he sold it to and turn the stadium into a casino.

In Benton Harbor, the same story - this former manufacturing center for Whirlpool with a nearly 100% Black population had a public park and beach on Lake Michigan until the Emergency Financial Manager stripped power from the mayor and city council who had long opposed selling the park and sold it to developers of a private golf course. The public park is now the Jack Nicklaus Signature Design Golf Course.

Detroit's newly installed EFM is Kevyn Orr, a bankruptcy lawyer with an east coast law firm, Jones Day. This firm's clients are the some of the largest banks involved in the LIBOR interest rate-rigging scandal. It was discovered that banks have been falsely inflating or deflating their rates so as to profit from trades, or to give the impression that they were more creditworthy than they were. LIBOR underpins approximately $350 trillion in derivatives. In the words of Professor Andrew Lo of MIT: "the scale of the scandal dwarfs by orders of magnitude any financial scam in the history of markets."

One of Jones Day's clients is the UBS bank which has already admitted to wrong-doing in the LIBOR scandal and paid a $1.5 billion fine to the US Department of Justice. UBS is the main bank holding a loan made to the City of Detroit in 2004 to cover pension obligations to city workers.

Many cities have been saddled with loans made by LIBOR banks and have been paying interest on loans fraudulently set. A number of municipalities, unions, pension funds and others are suing to recoup the inflated interest money. Will Detroit join in the lawsuits? It is highly doubtful now that Kevyn Orr is in control. He resigned from the Jones Day firm the day before he was appointed Detroit's EFM but Jones Day will the consulting law firm in the restructuring of Detroit's debt. Orr will directly supervise five of his former law firm partners including his former boss.

It is expected that the restructuring plan for Detroit will include selling off Belle Isle, the park island in the middle of the Detroit River outside of the downtown area, and other public assets like the Detroit Water and Sewage Department.

Detroit and other Michigan cities are undergoing the same austerity as others around the country such as Stockton, CA and Scranton, PA.

Black Workers a Key Factor

What distinguishes Michigan's cities is the fact that they are the heart of the Black working class where a united working class movement blazed the trail for unionization of industrial workers largely under left leadership in the 1930s and 40s.

Unions, churches and community organizations have been mobilizing protests against the takeover -the Council of Baptist Pastors of Detroit, the National Action Network, Rainbow PUSH, the NAACP, AFSCME and the UAW are mobilizing opposition. Lawsuits have been filed to challenge the takeover arguing constitutional grounds in the violation of election law, voting rights and the Governor's disregard of the majority vote to repeal the Emergency Financial Manager law on the ballot in November 2012 which won by 53% of the people statewide.

The takeover of Michigan cities is not the only part of the corporate agenda. The same week that Detroit was brought under dictatorial rule, the state's Right to Work law went into effect. In advance of the date, teacher unions around the state successfully bargained multi-year collective bargaining agreements that locked in dues or agency fee as a condition of employment, forestalling the impact of RTW under threats from the Governor to cut funding to any school district or university that signed the agreements. The Republican legislature is working on even more ways to reduce the power of public-sector unions by banning "exclusivity clauses" for public sector unions, i.e., withdrawing recognition that a union is the sole representative of a bargaining unit.

Reactionary Menu

The right wing Republican Michigan Legislature is brewing up an entire menu of reactionary laws. It includes prohibiting cities from passing paid sick leave ordinances to thwart a national movement that has won victories elsewhere; a ban on domestic partnership benefits; changing the method of counting Electoral College votes from winner-take-all to apportioning by congressional district, a measure designed to weaken the Black vote; bills to require drug tests and school attendance for children 16 and under as a condition for receiving food stamps.

Michigan has mandatory life sentences without parole for 360 children, most of whom are Black. No other country in the world puts their youth in prison.

Michigan is the playbook for the GOP in midwestern states in the 2014 and 2016 elections. The plan is to discourage the Black vote by stripping Black elected representatives of power and increase the white vote in the state with appeals to racism by blaming Black people and their representatives for "irresponsible" government.

This is austerity US style and it is coming down sharpest on the Black population and electorate while impacting all working people. It is an audacious roll back of the New Deal in the heart of the Black working class. The Left has an important role to play in educating about who is really to blame and helping to build a popular front against finance capital and its corporatist reactionary agenda. We are in a global struggle against finance capital no different in the US than in Cyprus, Greece, Portugal, and Spain.

There are a number of important arenas where demands against austerity and for jobs can be felt:

1) Campaigns to organize low-wage workers continue to grow. In April, 400 fast food workers conducted a second round of one day strikes in New York City, and the strike spread to Chicago with 500 demanding $15 an hour wages. WalMart workers staged a shop floor action in 100 stores around the country. These struggles are building coalitions of unions, community, civil rights, religious organizations and elected officials.

2) The UAW Nissan organizing drive in Canton, Mississippi, with a majority African American workforce, is using the same Civil Rights Trade Unionism strategy that won democratic victories in the 1930s and the 1950s/60s. As part of this effort, the Mississippi Student Justice Alliance organized a tour to three Historically Black Colleges and Universities with Danny Glover to build support, forming the Concerned Students for a Better Nissan.

3) Immigrant rights marches will build on the large rally in Washington DC in early April that brought together a rainbow of organizations and movements. May Day rallies around the country will highlight and press for just immigration reform and this will continue in the coming months until Congress acts.

4) The upcoming March on Washington in August will mark the 50th anniversary of the history-making march in 1963 that called for jobs and
freedom. As Bill Fletcher wrote in his Black Commentator column, we
need to go beyond celebrating and renew the call for jobs and freedom,
"bringing those demands into the 21st century by emphasizing issues
that include voting rights plus genuine economic development, peace
and planetary survival."

The crises of the climate, the economy and war are interrelated and as
socialists we understand the nature of the attack. As Mark Solomon,
CCDS Co-Chair Emeritus, wrote in his recent article, "Wither the Socialist
Left?" what is needed is an advanced, effective political instrument that
can forge the linkages between the economic crisis, the environmental
crisis and the crisis of militarism and war. The urgency is the deepening
crisis of capitalism. It requires bold steps and political will to build a left
that can have a powerful, lasting impact on the struggle for justice, peace
and a socialist future.

*Abridged Remarks presented 4/14/13 to the National Coordinating Com-
mittee, CCDS*

Whither the Socialist Left? Thinking the 'Unthinkable'

Historian Mark Solomon looks at
the prospects for a new socialist left

By Mark Solomon
Published by Portside March 6, 2013

On February 4, 2010 The Gallup Poll released
its latest data on the public's political atti-
tudes. The headline read: "Socialism Viewed
Positively by 36% of Americans." While the poll
did not attempt the daunting task of exploring
what a diverse public understood socialism to
mean, it nevertheless revealed an unmistak-
ably sympathetic image of a system that had been pilloried for generations by all of capitalism's dominant instruments of learning and information as well as by its power to suppress and slander socialist ideas and
organization.

In sheer numbers, that means a population at the teen-age level and
above of tens of millions with a favorable view of socialism.

Why then is the organized socialist movement in the United States so
small and so clearly wanting in light of the potential for building its numbers and influence?

That is a crucial question. At every major juncture in the history of the
country, radical individuals and organizations in advance of the mainstream have played essential roles in influencing, guiding and consoli-
dating broad currents for social change. In the revolution that birthed
this country, radical activists articulated demands from the grass roots
for an uncompromising and transforming revolution to crush colonial
oppression. Black and white abolitionists fought to make the erasure of
slavery the core objective of the Civil War while also linking that struggle
to women's suffrage and trade unionism. A mass Socialist Party in the
early 20th century fought for state intervention to combat the ravages of

an increasingly exploitative economic system while advancing the vision of a socialist commonwealth. In the Great Depression, the Communist Party and its allies fought the devastations of the crisis - helping to build popular movements to expand democracy, grow industrial unions and defend protections for labor embodied in the historic New Deal.

Small left and socialist organizations in the sixties supported a range of progressive struggles from peace to civil rights to women's liberation to gay rights and beyond. The limited resources of those groups were effective in galvanizing massive peace demonstrations and in campaigns against racist and sexist oppression. But the Cold War and McCarthyism had eviscerated any hope for a major influential socialist current. Consequently, no large and impacting force existed to extend to the peace movement a coherent anti-imperial analysis that might have contributed to its continuity and readiness to confront the wars of the nineties and the new century. Nor was there a strong socialist organization to contribute to the civil rights struggle by advocating for reform joined to a commitment to deeper social transformation. Had such a current existed, it might have contributed to building a broad protective barrier against the devastating FBI and local police violence against sectors of the movement like the Black Panthers.

There should be little debate today on the left over the need for a strong socialist voice and movement in light of festering economic stagnation, war on the working class, looming environmental catastrophe, a widening chasm between the super-rich and the rest of us, massive joblessness and incarceration savaging African Americans and other oppressed nationalities, crises in health care, housing and education. Such a strong socialist presence could offer a searching analysis of the present situation, help stimulate a broad public debate on short term solutions and formulate a vision of a socialist future that could begin to reach the minds and hearts of the 36 percent who claim to be sympathetic to that vision.

Why No Large Socialist Groups Today?

Back to the question: why is there no large respected socialist organization today? The answer is complex and not readily subject to a consensus. The failures of the first socialist wave in the 20th century, the unrelenting demonization of socialism by the dominant political apparatus, internal sectarian cultures and narrow social composition that inhibit outreach to youth and oppressed nationalities - have all contributed to a weak socialist presence.

Doubtless, some if not all, existing socialist organizations would insist that they are growing, respected and effective. That can be argued, but it is valid to acknowledge that existing socialist groups, to one degree or another, have made and continue to make important contributions to the struggle for a just present and better future. This is especially true of the work of individual socialists in various unions and mass organizations. However, the small size and inadequate resources of socialist organization nearly fatally inhibit their impact and influence. No matter how hard-working and principled, small socialist groups are drowned out by the power and pervasiveness of the dominant tools of information and education. The Internet has opened a window to reaching mass audiences. But socialist websites (if one is successful in locating them) cannot substitute for the indispensable task of organizational outreach, of human beings making direct contact with other human beings, of physical debate and discussion, of well-orchestrated, highly visible mass actions. The time has come to work for the convergence of socialist organizations committed to non-sectarian democratic struggle, engagement with mass movements, and open debate in search of effective responses to present crises and to projecting a socialist future.

There are socialist organizations already airing divergent views within their ranks - reflecting positions that overlap with other socialist organizations committed to democratic struggle and socialist education. The Committees of Correspondence for Democracy and Socialism, the Communist Party USA, Democratic Socialists of America and the Freedom Road Socialist Organization have been meeting to explore areas for cooperation in advancing the fight to defend the needs and interests of all working people. With involvement of their members, and with all who honestly wish a unity project to succeed, those organizations could constitute a starting point for other left and socialist groups and individuals to join as equal participants in building an imaginative, revitalized socialist presence.

A conversation with a veteran socialist historian about merger brought a nearly apoplectic response: that will never happen; too much history of mutual antagonism; too much institutional self-aggrandizement; too much belief within each organization of their ideological and strategic "certainties," etc.

His bleak assessment may well be valid. One could list even more problems: the comfort of organizational silos, the complexity of sorting out and merging the physical resources of each organization, selecting a conjoined leadership, lingering political and ideological differences.

It can also be argued that a merger of organizations with a combined membership of a few thousand would still not be large or vibrant enough to make an impact on a country of over 300 million; nor would its combined membership include a sufficient component of youth, African Americans, Latinos, Asians, etc., commensurate with the country's changing demographics.

That perhaps misses a crucial point. While growth and dynamism are not guaranteed, the open-minded and comradely spirit embodied in a merger could excite and inspire thousands of former members of those organizations to join a new, collaborative entity. Many others impressed by a revitalized commitment by socialists to put aside narrow interests and seek common ground could also be moved to join. The simple declaration of unity and amalgamation by old ideological foes will stir an energized, hopeful response on the left.

Among socialist organizations there is a long tradition of opposition to racism, sexism and homophobia; a concrete record of unwavering struggle for racial and gender justice as indispensable to all working class aspirations. With that experience and consciousness, a renewed socialist organization with augmented resources would have the potential to speak directly to young people of color, to the jailed and formerly jailed, to a new generation of students, to teen aged youth, to the large numbers who joined the Occupy movement, the unaffiliated leftists and socialists who have joined the rapidly growing Jacobin journal, Labor Notes, the large Left Forums, the Left Labor Project, etc. Whatever its initial form, an alliance of socialists offers the promise of a continuous, enduring framework for democratic struggle, for discussion, for debate, for learning, for growing - all within a stable, political and organizational environment.

With a visible presence for outreach to emerging but undefined left forces, a merged socialist movement could presumably generate the financial resources to hire and train young organizers. With stronger organization derived from convergence, it could tap latent left and socialist sentiment in "red states," especially the South and Midwest that would reawaken the truly national presence of socialism that characterized the Socialist Party in the early 20th century.

Those augmented resources could open up space for expanded socialist education through debate and discussion, through a combination of new publications and continuing publications of the merged organizations, through classes, think tanks and through utilization of the Internet. The present Online University of the Left is an excellent example of the potential for utilization on a large scale of new technology for socialist education.

Despite the enormous challenges inherent in convergence, there are a number of reasons to anticipate readiness for unified socialist organizing:

1. First and foremost, the present crisis of world capitalism is systemic. While there will continue to be economic peaks and valleys, the overall prognosis is for enervation and stagnation that will increasingly demon-

strate capitalism's declining ability to provide decent lives for present and future generations.

2. There is likely agreement among various organizations on the need for a long-range socialist transformation. There is a likely consensus on the validity of Marx's basic critique of the contradictions inherent in capitalism: increasingly socialized production colliding with private appropriation of the fruits of that production - constituting the key source of the system's inherent instability. Historically, the relations of production (manifested in social classes) become fetters upon the productive forces (human beings and machinery) - thus requiring the overturning of the old system - socializing the relations of production in order to bring them into harmony with highly socialized productive forces. With globalization of capital that contradiction between social production and private appropriation has itself become global - resulting in the accumulation of unimaginable wealth by a small minority while masses languish in deepening poverty and social misery.

3. There is likely agreement that both the path to socialism and its essential character are subjects for study, debate and experimentation. There is much to study: the "solidarity economy" posits 21st century socialism with workers' control of all essential institutions, a market function and imperative ecological concern. There are a growing number of experiments in cooperatives, workers' self-management, and local public ownership of energy. Other approaches stress confrontation with corporate power through mass struggle for control of state policy - aiming to expand the public sphere while reducing and eventually eliminating corporate control of the economy and society. In sum, a new socialist organization will open avenues to fresh, challenging exploration of social transformation.

4. There is a likely consensus among socialists that "vanguard" organizations and sectarian "cadre" groups have been negated by the existence of a broadly heterogeneous multiracial working class of women and men. The present-day working class and its allies are too diverse to be led by a single, narrowly conceived political current. A renewed socialist organization must reflect that heterogeneity as well as the determination of members to be full, controlling participants in present struggles and in charting a socialist future. The new organization's structure would likely be neither fully "vertical" nor fully "horizontal." In the past the former has often undermined democratic participation and the latter (illustrated by the experience of the Occupy movement) has often led to organizational incoherence and stasis.

5. There is likely agreement that there should be no preexisting standard for socialist organizing that mandates a "take it or leave it" rigidity.

The door should be open to experimentation in exploring both organizational and theoretical issues. There is also likely agreement for the short-and-medium-term at least that a converged organization should not be formed as party or electoral organization. The electoral issue, a major point of contention on the left, could be a major topic of exploration and debate. There should be no obstacles for those who sincerely wish to join the struggle against the ravages of the system and who seek a socialist alternative. In that regard it is important to note the variety of left and socialist movements around the world worthy of study.

No Single Path

Clearly, there is no single "correct" path to 21st century socialism. Greece, in the midst of existential crisis, has given rise to Syriza, merging a remarkable range of organizations despite sharply different ideological and historical roots into a unified party whose platform rejects austerity, demands the cancellation of Greece's debt and reform of the European Central Bank. Syriza emerged in 2001 from a group called "Space for Dialogue for the Unity and Common Action of the Left." In June 2012, Syriza received almost 27% of the vote in parliamentary elections, making it the main opposition party and positioning it as the potential future governing party.

In France, a coalition of left and socialist parties has formed a Left-Front coalition that ran a unified campaign in the last national elections. Germany has "Die Linke," the Left Party formed from a coalition of the successors to the old ruling party in the German Democratic Republic and a militant West German labor organization. An all-European Left Party is a continental formation of an impressive array of left and socialist parties and organizations.

Latin America is perhaps the region with the greatest left and socialist experimentation that generally stresses democratic and participatory engagement at the grass roots in building alternatives to capitalism. The Latin American left in particular has advanced some of the most compelling interpretations of Marx's thinking concerning the crucial issues of ecological preservation and survival. It has also engendered, country-by-country a variety of social experiments based upon distinct national conditions involving various degrees of mixed, transitional economies on the road to socialism.

Speaking only for myself, I would like to see the creation of an entirely new organization. However, a total merger of organizations at this time can justly be viewed as utopian at best and naïve at worst. One must acknowledge the need for a patient process - for ongoing consultation, for gradual building of mutual comfort and mutual confidence, for a possible stage of confederation or alliance. Crucially, joint activities to defeat austerity and the right wing offensive constitute a sound basis at this juncture on the road to convergence. In the long term, the next generation and generations beyond will determine the form and content of the struggle for social transformation based on changed circumstances that cannot now be fully envisioned.

That does not negate the need for "all deliberate speed" in building an advanced, effective political instrument to help forge the linkages between the economic crisis, the environmental crisis and the crisis of militarism and war. That instrument is needed to help provide political depth and interconnectedness to burgeoning movements on the environment, immigration, gun control, women's rights, the prison-industrial complex, voting rights, student debt, protection of Social Security and Medicare, jobs and union rights, and the struggle against interventionism and the national security state. Above all, the urgency of the deepening crisis of capitalism demands the political will of socialist organizations to take those bold and resolute steps to forming a strong new alliance capable of having a powerful and lasting impact on the struggle for justice, peace and a socialist future.

Mark Solomon is past national co-chair of the United States Peace Council and the Committees of Correspondence for Democracy and Socialism. He is author of The Cry Was Unity: Communists and African Americans, 1917-1936, and is currently working on a memoir/narrative at the Du Bois Institute at Harvard University on the freedom and peace movements in the 1940s and 1950s.

Beyond 2012: Advancing a Progressive Coalition

By Harry Targ

Workers are marching in New York City, Boston, Chicago, and San Francisco for their rights. Activists for women's rights, gay rights, and the rights of people of color are on the move. Environmentalists are saying "no" Tar Sands and "yes" to moving nationally and globally against the dangers of climate change.

Everyone is demanding that the Obama Administration reject demands by the rightwing to cut Medicare, Medicaid, and Social Security while protecting tax breaks for the rich and excessive military spending.

Millions of us worked to defeat the far rightwing in the 2012 elections and celebrated the historic reelection of an African American for President. During much of Obama's first term, the President sought to compromise with the rightwing, avoiding radical reforms; for example the one that would have provided Americans with single payer health care. He was reluctant to defend American public institutions, such as schools and libraries, worker's rights, and to demand adequate resources for rebuilding our physical infrastructure and saving our environment.

However, in President Obama's 2013 inaugural address he affirmed his commitment to social and economic justice, peace, and protection of our precious and threatened environment. The president referred metaphorically to Seneca Falls, Selma, and Stonewall to underscore his commitment to women, African-Americans, and gays and lesbians. While he should have added Flint, Michigan, site of worker sit-downs in 1937 where rights to organize where demanded, Obama clearly promised to work toward empowerment of some of the traditionally voiceless, usually not referred to in inaugural speeches. Obama also raised in a forceful way the problem of climate change. The President, without raising specifics, clearly articulated a progressive agenda for the next four years that we on the left should organize around.

In addition, there are signs that the Obama election organization is being transformed into what could become part of a social movement to support a progressive agenda in the Congress. Organizing for Action (OFA) promises to take the resources, human and financial, that were mobilized during the campaign to build constituencies to work on issues and campaigns in Congressional districts. Skeptics correctly suggest that OFA may serve more to channel and control growing militancy at the grassroots rather than unleash it. However, those of us at the base can use the OFA format and resources as part of our own organizing.

Organizing at the grassroots in communities and states is particularly critical in the thirty states in which government is dominated by Tea Party and other conservative elected officials. And it is in these states and communities that outside money has poured in to reverse institutions and policies that service human needs. In many of the states, such as Indiana, advocates for reaction have gained an upper hand and threaten public institutions, social programs, and democratic representation.

Wrong Step in 2008

We, the left/liberal community, stepped back from activism after the 2008 election assuming that the new President would advance a people's agenda. We were wrong. He adopted a cautious and pragmatic strategy incorrectly assuming he could achieve compromise policies with Republicans and Blue Dog Democrats. In 2010, a new group of Republicans opposed to virtually all public institutions, the so-called Tea Party Republicans, gained many seats in Congress, state legislatures, and governorships.

In the 2012 elections the same progressive forces which withdrew from political combat after 2008 and sat out the 2010 elections, mobilized to reelect the President in 2012. Since last November they have proclaimed that they will not become passive again.
We must stand for human progress inside the legislative/executive arena and everywhere in the public sphere. We must stand up for the populist agenda candidate Obama proposed in 2008 and was hesitant to deliver and he has articulated in his 2013 inaugural speech.

In short, we in labor, women's, African-American, Latino, environmental, and civil liberties groups must build a coalition that recognizes that we share common needs and goals. We must realize we are all victims of an economic and political system that rewards the few at the expense of the many.

How do we come together? How should we relate to the electoral arena, in our communities and states? Should we work in the Democratic Party? A progressive segment of it and/or a Third Party? When and where should we protest? Can we begin to construct alternative institutions? How can we spread our messages through the media--print, electronic, public performance?

Perhaps most important is the question of our vision of the future. What kind of society would we want to create? How can we achieve economic and political justice for all?

These are heady questions but they can only be answered if we act together. As inspired by the Rebuild the American Dream campaigns and Occupy movements of 2011 we can begin to dialogue anew about building movements in our communities, identifying a range of issues to work on together, and, ultimately advancing our states and society toward economic and social justice.

Harry Targ is a professor of Peace Studies at Purdue, a CCDS National Committee member, and editor of this journal.

Toward a Progressive Southern Strategy

By Janet Tucker
CCDS National Coordinator

On Labor Day 2012 labor organizations and activists, civil rights and
immigrant rights organizations met
in Charlotte, NC and formed the
Southern Workers Assembly. This
was initiated by Black Workers for
Justice in North Carolina. They have
a long history of work in North Carolina including working in the "North
Carolina by the Historic Thousands
on Jones Street" coalition, which is
led by the state-level affiliates of
the NAACP, AFL-CIO and National
Council of Churches. Together with
their allies, they have been instru-
mental in winning major organizing victories in North Carolina; for
example, the recent labor victory at

the world's largest hog slaughterhouse in Tar Heel, NC, where the United
Food and Commercial Workers finally won a National Labor Relations
Board election after fighting years of intimidation by Smithfield Foods.

This is a really exciting development for the South. The banner on their
website reads "Building a Southern Labor Alliance: Call to Action to Organize Labor in the South." The South has a rich history of labor organizing
but the South also has been a stronghold of reaction, and labor remains
largely unorganized. The cited Labor Day meeting was followed up with
a second meeting in Charleston, SC in December, 2012.

Jaribu Hill from the Mississippi Workers Center for Human Rights had
this to say: "The Southern Workers' Assembly is long overdue! It is absolutely the most important gathering of workers' rights organizers,
and human rights defenders. As we watch the political footballs being
passed from one side of the aisle to the other, we know that working

people must take power. We cannot rely upon any part of the decaying machine that rolls over the hopes and aspirations of millions of workers and their families, while greasing the cogs of profit and exploitation. We must stand together, assemble, plan, organize and win!"

Ken Riley, President of South Carolina AFL-CIO added, "This year, the state was trying to strengthen the Right-to-Work laws. Everything that was originally in there that was very harmful got stripped from the bill. It first passed the House, but when it got back to the Senate, we were there to express our concerns and raise issues of legality and constitutionality."

In Canton, Mississippi workers struggle to organize a union at the Nissan auto plan where 70% of the 3,300 workers are black. The union sees a winning strategy in depicting the right to unionize freely, as a basic civil right. "The civil rights experience was fought on that very ground," said Gary Casteel, the UAW's top official in the US South. "We've been saying that worker rights is the civil rights battle of the 21st century."

In April students from the Mississippi Student Justice Alliance (MSJA) organized "Concerned Students for a Better Nissan College Tour." These youth-led tours of surrounding Historically Black Colleges and Universities spread the message of justice for the Nissan workers. While meeting with students in Tennessee they also met with some Nissan workers, including some from a plant in Smyrna, TN.

Worker Centers Spreading Across the South

These struggles are not happening in isolation. Workers Centers are actively engaged across the South from Florida to Mississippi to North Carolina. For example the Miami Workers Center took an active role in the 2012 elections with the Florida New Majority, while also working around community and labor issues.

In his presentation on Organizing the South at the CCDS 6th National Convention in 2009, Zach Robinson began with a brief definition of the Southern region of the United States. "The Southern region consists of the 11 states of the former confederacy, plus the two border states of Kentucky and Missouri. The common history I mentioned is, of course, the history of slavery and of the struggle for freedom of the African-American people. To quote William Faulkner, "'The past is not dead; it's not even past.'"

While progressives rejoice in Romney's defeat in the 2012 elections, we must look what happened in the South to know how true Faulkner's statement is. This nation was built on white supremacy which was based in the South, the home of slavery. Since the overthrow of reconstruction the right keeps reinventing itself. With recent redistricting and gerrymandering there is a solid Republican block across the South.

The South: Red or Purple?

With the exceptions of Virginia and Florida, the southern states were solidly red in the 2012 elections. Of course this does not tell the whole picture. The South is seeing changing demographics just like the rest of the nation. Chris Kromm states in his article The Changing Face of Southern Voters, "in 2012, 18.6 million Southerners in 13 states voted for President Obama -- about 45 percent of Southern voters -- compared to 22.6 million for Romney." So may we call the South "purple"?

In all southern states with the exception of Kentucky, both the state houses and senates are controlled by the Republican Party, a result of gerrymandering after the 2010 census.   Southern states are among those with the lowest union membership. In most southern states public workers, even when represented by a union, are denied the right to collective bargaining. All southern states are right-to-work states with the exception of Kentucky—a trend that is spreading across the country.

A new analysis by the Institute for Southern Studies looked at the effect of gerrymandering in the south. There is a significant mismatch between voters' choices and who represents them in Congress than in the rest of the nation.

Districts Designed to Help GOP

Chris Kromm also points out in another article, "As Republicans have come to dominate Southern state legislatures, they have seized the opportunity to design districts which are particularly effective at minimizing the ability of Democrats to compete in Congressional races. As a result, the gap between the number of voters who vote Democratic for Congress and the actual number of Democratic representatives who will take office this month is four times greater in the South than the national average - a situation that exaggerates the power of Republicans in the South and fuels perceptions of the region as a monolithic conservative stronghold."

It's useful to compare the maps on the following page:

Slavery, 1859   ## Racial segregation, 1950

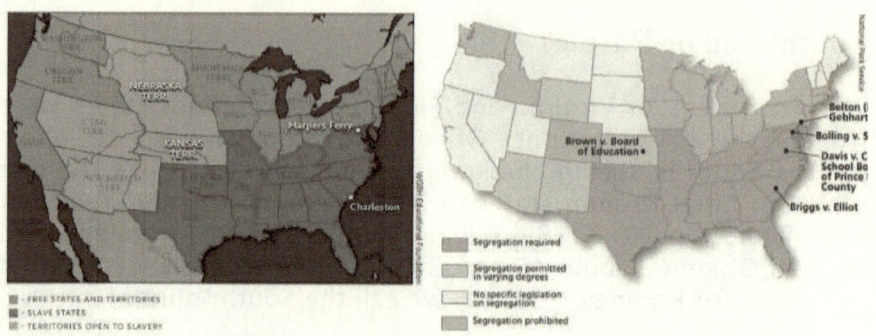

Presidential election, 2012

And these 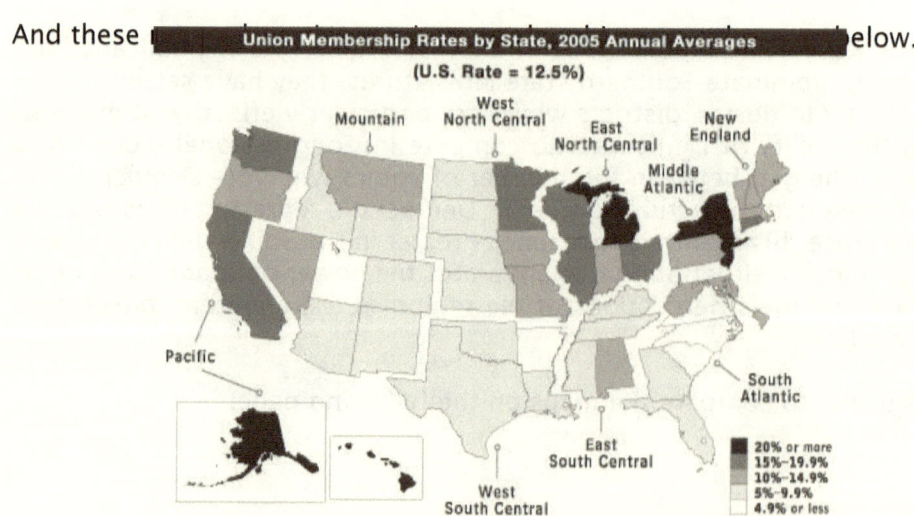 below.

Source: Current Population Survey, Bureau of Labor Statistics. Web: www.bls.gov/news.release/pdf/union2.pdf

So we have a solid block of Republican rule in the South defying democracy and at the same time continuing infringement and threats to voting rights.

'The past is not dead; it's not even past.'

In his book "Where Do We Go from Here?" Dr. Martin Luther King, Jr. put it this way:

"Since before the Civil War, the alliance of Southern racism and northern reaction has been the major roadblock to all social advancement. The cohesive political structure of the South working through this alliance enabled a minority of the population to imprint its ideology on the nation's laws. This explains why the United States is still far behind European nations in all forms of social legislation. England, France, Germany, Sweden, all distinctly less wealthy than us, provide more security relatively for their people."

So really "Where Do We Go from Here?" What can history teach us? What are our tasks in 2013?

In Civil Rights Unionism, Robert Korstad wrote about the struggle to organize tobacco workers in North Carolina at RJ Reynolds. This is an amazing part of the South's history. By 1940 RJ Reynolds had become the largest tobacco manufacturer in the world. There were 12,000 employees and several thousand seasonal workers. This manufacturer had one of the largest concentrations of industrial workers in the region. Two-thirds were African American and over half were women. After a long and patient process of union organizing the situation changed overnight.

That change happened on a June morning in 1942. Theodosia Simpson, a worker, explained what happened, "The lady who worked on the machine next to me, she was a widow with 5 kids, and she was sick that day. ... She couldn't keep up with her work. .... The foreman came up and told her that if she didn't catch up, 'there was the door the carpenter left'. She started crying because she had these children to rear and nobody working but her." This was spurred on by the death on the line of a 38 year old man who had been sick for several days. And thus the sit down strike started in Plant Number 65. This rapidly spread to other plants accompanied with rapid increase in union membership. Through this the FTA (Food, Tobacco, Agriculture and Allied Workers of America) Local 22 was formed. The sit down strike was joined by a few hundred whites. About 3000 whites continued to work.

"On Thursday morning, June 17, no one could have predicted what occurred over the next six days but by Wednesday June 23rd, there seemed no way to stop what had been put in motion. The willingness of thousands of black workers to walk off their jobs with some risk to themselves and their families represented a rare and remarkable moment in southern history. The walkout, the rapid membership drive, and the mass meetings gave reason for hope. Out of such hope Local 22 was born" (Korstat).

Along with fighting for better working conditions, Local 22 was active politically. They fought against Black exclusion from politics and social services. They registered thousands of Black voters and revitalized the local NAACP chapter, demanding a greater voice in city government. In 1948 the FTA directed their energies to the Progressive Party and the presidential campaign of Henry Wallace. The Black churches played an integral and supporting role here. They housed many meetings. Church committees that involved many of the workers, mostly women, served as a great training ground for union leaders.

Civil Rights Unionism

As Zach Robinson stated in his report Organizing the South, "The union's unique strategic outlook united its workplace organizing efforts with community and church-based organizations. It fought for a different kind of community, one where broad racial injustices could be redressed. In conjunction with community organizations, it organized campaigns for literacy and voter registration resulting in the election of Kenneth Williams as Winston-Salem Alderman, the first African-American to serve in this position since Reconstruction."

Operation Dixie was the effort by the CIO to organize workers in the South following World War II. The CIO leadership realized that the unorganized South would have a negative effect on the whole labor movement especially as plants moved south to flee organized labor in the North. Barbara Griffith documented in Crisis of American Labor and the defeat of the CIO in 194,6 that with the investment of $1,000,000 and 250 organizers, the CIO initiated Operation Dixie as a "holy crusade". This effort failed bitterly. Operation Dixie officially ended in 1953 but Griffith states that the campaign failed in its first 6 months.

There are a number of opinions as to why it failed. Some say it may not have been possible during that particular period of history. But it is hardly so simple. They faced difficult conditions for sure. "Indeed, the campaign is more a study in the techniques of union-busting than union-building," wrote Michael Honey in his review of Griffith's book.

The CIO failed to have a good analysis of concrete conditions; one was misjudging the harsh conditions that existed in the South for union organizing. Anne Braden spoke of the "police state" that existed in the South until broken by the 1960's. Michael Honey went on to write, "Southern workers were intimidated and harassed from all sides. ... Christian fundamentalists flooded factory workers with anti-communist publications. Preachers, newspaper editors, politicians, and police, along with law firms specializing in union-busting, joined in a 'cultural war' against CIO unions as thugs and vigilantes beat up organizers. Company officials used every method at their disposal to make workers fearful to take a leaflet, attend a meeting, or speak to an organizer. Wiretaps, threatening phone calls, racial innuendos, quick arrests and brutal sentences for organizers (which included prison and work on road gangs), sudden lockouts, firings of union members, and employer threats that they would shut down rather than allow unionization, all were used to generate fear among southern workers." In speaking to this same point Bill Fletcher, Jr. stated, "The South was viewed by the CIO too much as simply another geographic region, not as agro-political region which contained a large African-American population"

In addition, the failure was caused by a flawed understanding of the changing conditions in the US. "Yet the end of the Second World War was also a point when the United States successfully asserted its hegemony over the Western world and in so doing chose to break its wartime alliance with the USSR. This was coupled with the crushing of domestic progressive movements. Operation Dixie fell right into the center of this changing environment and was affected by it." Bill Fletcher in A Campaign That Failed, a review of Griffith's book for Monthly Review, 1990. But the most serious errors were internal to the CIO itself. First, it failed to see the centrality of fighting racism in organizing the South and failed to appreciate the leading role of black workers. Secondly the CIO fell prey to red baiting, purging their ranks of communist organizers. These errors sealed the defeat of Operation Dixie.

Robert Korstad states in Civil Rights Unionism, "the CIO officials saw white textile workers as the key to organizing the South, not only because textiles were the region's largest single industry ... but also because the textile union was Operation Dixie's largest financial backer. Assuming, as they did, that white textile workers were irredeemably racist and that they would respond only to the most cautious and narrowly defined appeals, Operation Dixie's leaders took pains to play down the CIO's strength in the black community, hired few Black organizers, and avoided any linkage between unionization and civil rights."

According to Michael Honey, "Although production workers in the textile industry, by employer design, were nearly all white, Blacks often made up a majority in sawmills, furniture, tobacco and cotton processing factories, and a significant portion of the work force in steel, coal, iron ore, and other enterprises. Outside of textiles, unionization depended on black and white cooperation

There are some positive examples. In many cases, where organizing was successful, it was because the unions spearheading the organizing cam-paigns were led by leftists, especially members and supporters of the Communist Party (CP). "The Communists had a deeper understanding of what was required to win in the South than many other organizers," said Paul Krehbiel, a union organizer in the south in the mid-1980's. "Organizers needed a clear understanding of the necessity of building class unity, and that means consistently opposing racism, and finding ways to unite Black and white workers. Organizers also need tenacity, creativity, and a well thought-out organizing plan to build the union and win an election. And, when they can involve the community, their chances of success increase substantially." One example was the FTA (Food, Tobacco, Agriculture and allied workers of America).

Social Revolution

FTA Union President, Donald Henderson, said in his report to the 1947 convention, "It cannot be emphasized too much that the Southern Drive is more than a mere organizing campaign. It is in fact a social revolu-tion." Korstad goes on to say, "A social revolution is not what the CIO leaders had in mind....They did little to support it and viewed it less as a jewel in their crown than a liability".

But some unions did embrace social justice unionism, and class unity – some might call that a "social revolution." One was the United Furniture Workers Union (UFWA), the union Krehbiel worked for in the mid-1980s. Founded in 1937 by the Communist-led Furniture Workers Industrial Union, the UFWA had Communists and CP supporters in its leadership right from its founding, according to Daniel Cornfield in his book about the UFWA, Becoming a Mighty Voice. The union had its largest mem-bership base in New York City and other regions in the northeast and mid-west. But, UFWA leaders immediately turned their sites toward organizing the South, because of the very large number of furniture workers located there, and because they understood the importance of organizing the largely non-union South. The UFWA leaders also knew that they would have to tackle racism, and work hard to build class and racial unity.

After years of developing good organizing possibilities and laying the ground work for a union organizing campaign, the UFWA won a big victory at nine Thomasville Chair Company plants in North Carolina in 1946. The nine plants employed 1,200 workers, a third of whom were Black. The UFWA, from the very beginning, worked to build multi-racial unity among the Black and white workers at Thomasville. They knew this was essential if they were going to win. The campaign was brutal, but the union won after a 17-week strike, and a racially integrated group of over 3,000 people -- workers, their families, and community supporters -- marched through town. The victory was big, with a 817-335 vote.

The UFWA targeted other non-union furniture companies in southern states for union organizing campaigns. North Carolina alone had over 40,000 furniture workers during this period, comprising one of the largest concentrations of furniture workers anywhere.

Michael Honey states "Conservatism, Griffith points out, was characteristic of whites, not Blacks, who were 'highly politicized' and ready to organize in the postwar period. Employer manipulation of fundamentalist religion and anti-communism as methods of undermining unionization worked almost exclusively among whites. Most Black workers rejected anticommunism as a segregationist code word for racial mixing, which it was, and used religion as a pro-union ideology of solidarity".

While the UFWA was working to win more organizing victories in the South, the political tide was turning in the country. The big gains that many unions made from the national strike wave of 1946 and big organizing victories of that period, scared employers, racists, and the political right, and a reactionary backlash was launched.

Moderates Can Conciliate with Reactionaries

The moderates, conservatives, and racists in the labor movement, afraid of losing their influence to the emerging multi-racial, left and progressive-led forces, joined this reactionary movement. Along with the help from employers and the government, the moderates and conservatives in the labor movement embarked on a purge of leftist union leaders, and raided their members. Since these left leaders were the major advocates of multi-racial unity, when they were purged, the racist history of most unions was allowed to remain intact. This inherent racism in the CIO was part of an overall turn to the rights. Falling prey to red baiting gutted the CIO from the inside out.

Jack O'Dell spoke of his experience in this period in an interview with Sam Sills: "I came into the civil rights movement through the industrial trade union movement. I volunteered to be an organizer for Operation Dixie, which is what the CIO was into at that particular point and I helped to organize the hotel and restaurant workers over on the beach and so forth. ... Now, in the South what I was describing was a situation where we were outnumbered because the anti-Communist thing became a banner — a tent under which all these racist elements could assemble and cover their flanks. They teamed up with the police and the Klan, the Union officials, to run blacks out of the Union hall. It was almost like a Reconstruction thing you read about —how they overthrew the government, the blacks are forced to flee, and so forth. It was that kind of atmosphere they were able to create."

In the end, Reynolds workers in FTA Local 22 were defeated in what Korstad called a "metamorphosis of white supremacy." He went on to say, "In the end however, the breakup of the workers' movement in Winston-Salem and in the United States required an extraordinary feat of political repression. It was the post WWII red scare that finally silenced dissident voices and constrained political debate. Although the anti-Communist crusade singled out individuals and organizations, the real targets were the broad social movements begun in the 1930s."

Bill Fletcher also stated in his article that "the inability and unwillingness of organized labor to commit itself to a protracted effort to organize this region has had serious consequences for the possibilities of truly national progressive politics." Further, he states that there was no view of the strategic unity between the labor movement and the civil rights movement, "The history and development of Operation Dixie is so terribly ironic because it transpires precisely at the moment that forces were grouping together in the South to begin the protracted campaign against Jim Crow."

Jim Crow and Red Baiting

The UFWA was prepared to unite with a broader movement to end Jim Crow in the South. But, the McCarthy red-baiting fever of that period derailed the unions most likely to be involved. While the UFWA suffered some serious losses due to McCarthyism, it weathered the anti-communist witch-hunts better than most unions. Known Communists in the leadership of the UFWA left their national leadership positions – some were voted out mostly by non-communist liberals, to stop the red-baiting attacks on the UFWA. Significantly, other leaders and members, not known publicly for their leftist beliefs, were allowed to remain. Thus, the UFWA was able to maintain a liberal leadership throughout the McCarthy period. As the reactionary atmosphere waned in the late 1950s and 1960s to the fresh winds of the civil rights movement, the UFWA was already in step with the new political currents. The UFWA linked up early with the civil rights movement, and continued the union's progressive traditions into the 1970's and 1980's, and into its merger with a larger union in late 1986.

Paul Krehbiel, a long-time progressive trade unionist, was on staff with the UFWA in 1985 and 1986 in Nashville, Tennessee, where the UFWA had moved its national office in 1979 to focus on organizing the south. He said he saw that this progressive tradition was still intact in the UFWA. Krehbiel was the managing editor of the union's national newspaper, the Furniture Workers Press, and he assisted on union organizing campaigns in the south. He was assigned to work on a campaign at Pilliod Furniture Company in Meridian, Mississippi, which employed 400 workers, about 200 white and 200 Black. The campaign was under the direction of Willie Rudd, the dynamic Black Vice President for the Southern Region of the UFWA. Rudd was born in Mississippi and spent many years organizing there, as well as in other southern states.

One of Krehbiel's assignments was to contact other unions in the area to ask for their help in making audio tapes urging support for the UFWA organizing campaign at Pilliod. These tapes were then to be played on a popular radio program early in the morning when Pilliod workers drove to work.

When Rudd went over the lists of unions with Krehbiel, he told Krehbiel that he'd enjoying talking to the leaders of the local Woodworkers union in Meridian. Krehbiel asked why. Rudd told him they had been the leaders of the Ku Klux Klan there. Krehbiel asked why the UFWA would be contacting them.

Challenging the KKK in the Woodworkers

Rudd explained that several years earlier, the Woodworkers local union went on strike and were losing badly, Krehbiel said, recounting the story. The Woodworkers union had little public support because no one wanted to be seen challenging a big employer. So, Rudd and other UFWA members organized a big contingent of UFWA members, both Blacks and whites, to go to the Woodworkers picket-line to support their strike. The Woodworkers were stunned. But, as the members of both unions got to know each other on the picket line, many barriers came down. After the strike, the Woodworker union leaders quit the Klan.

When Krehbiel called the leader of the Woodworkers union, Dexter, as soon as Krehbiel mentioned that he was calling on behalf of Willie Rudd, Dexter said, "Whatever Willie Rudd wants you've got from me." Krehbiel said that Dexter made an audio tape encouraging Pilliod workers to join and vote for the UFWA in the upcoming election, and did everything else the UFWA asked of him.

The UFWA had majority support among the Black workers, though the union wanted to strengthen and expand it. But, many of the white workers still had not committed to the union, and it was crucial to win over many more of them to win the election. The radio ads that Dexter made helped, Krehbiel said, but the workers needed to talk face-to-face with union supporters. It was especially important that white union organizers talk directly to white Pilliod workers.

Krehbiel said he and other white organizers did house visits to white workers. "Many lived in very poor housing." "Some lived in small broken down trailers in open fields. I could see that many were afraid. They were living on the margins of survival, but they had been told all their lives they were better than Blacks. I had worked in a furniture factory, so that helped me connect with them. I had to convince them that all the workers at Pilliod, standing together as one, would create a large enough group to win the election and bring in the union. That, and only that, would give them a chance to begin to improve their lives. I told them that the union needed their vote."

As election day neared, the UFWA was winning more white workers to the union but they knew the vote would be close. Right before the election, the company put out a leaflet just to the white workers with a large photo of Willie Rudd speaking at a rally, with the caption: Do you want to take orders from this man? Vote No. "Racism reared its ugly head again," Krehbiel said. Pilliod promised the workers that management would address their complaints if the workers would give the company another chance by keeping the union out.

On election day, the union's observers reported that the votes were close as the ballots were counted and tallied, but at the finish the UFWA lost by just a handful of votes. Pilliod didn't resolve the workers complaints, and the UFWA went back the next year and won.

"The lessons were clear," Krehbiel said. "People who have backward ideas aren't necessarily wedded to these ideas forever. Under the right conditions, and with the right approach, they can change. The UFWA leadership, under Willie Rudd, showed the power of Black and white workers working together in a dramatic display of support for workers who previously scorned them. In this case, the Woodworkers union recognized that their interests as workers – their class interests, were more important than their ideas about race."

We have a strong history to draw on. It underlines the importance of unity of workers with the broader civil rights struggle and today the immigrant rights struggle. Strength comes from uniting shop floor struggles with community struggles. We need to be prepared to dig our heals in for a protracted struggle but as Dr. Martin Luther King, Jr. said, "The Arc of the Moral Universe Is Long, but It Bends Toward Justice"

Worker Empowerment: From Elections to Stewards Councils

By Paul Krehbiel

Labor and society benefit when rank-and-file workers are empowered.

The greatest worker empowerment in our nation's history came in the 1930s and 1940s when millions of workers organized huge strikes, and built and ran their own unions in response to the impoverishment of the Great Depression. They won dramatic improvements in wages, benefits and rights for all workers. Their political power helped establish minimum wage laws, weekends off, paid holidays, healthcare benefits, pensions, Social Security, job-creating government programs like the Works Progress Administration, unemployment insurance and other New Deal programs, and later, Medicare and Medicaid which are under fierce attack today by corporate and right-wing forces.

Behind this mass workers movement of the 1930s was organization. Spontaneous rebellions occurred, but without organized grassroots organizing which the general public rarely saw, the mass uprisings and big gains would have been fewer, shorter-lived, and weaker in content. The left, including Communists, provided much of this organization and leadership.

Today, there is ferment among the working class and in other sectors of society, but too much of it is unorganized, due to the unique problems we face today in 2013. These problems have roots that go back decades. First, the red-baiting McCarthyism of the 1950s forced most Communists and other left/progressive leaders out of union leadership, and out of many unions and other organizations, greatly weakening them. Second, the world economy has changed dramatically especially as competitors to US capital emerged. Deindustrialization of the 1970s, 1980s and beyond destroyed over 30 million jobs, creating permanently high unemployment. Since a significant number of lost jobs then were good union jobs, it seriously undermined already weakened unions -- the very unions that had led the workers movement of the Great Depression years.

Millions more jobs are being lost today, as the global capitalist economic crisis continues. The shifting of wealth from the working class to the major capitalists in the US and most other capitalist countries has reached such massive proportions that there currently isn't enough money in the broader society to meet people's needs. Political and other barriers have been erected to protect this shift of wealth. Since the economic meltdown of 2008, corporate profits are soaring, while millions of people suffer economic hardship. In the US, Black and Latino youth have been hardest hit, as they have been for generations, suffering 40%, 50% and higher chronic unemployment in many inner city neighborhoods. All of this is the normal functioning of capitalism.

Workers Fighting Back

Yet, people are resisting and fighting back. The most recent example nationally was the 2012 elections. An organized and massive opposition defeated those most responsible for the austerity push -- giant corporations and banks aligned with the Republican Party. Millions of people got actively involved in the 2012 elections, organized through the Democratic Party, unions, and many other organizations. Union workers made up one of the largest groups in this opposition.

For unions, it was clear that President Barack Obama should be re-elected on November 6, 2012. While Obama achieved some gains for working people in his first term, he missed the boat on other important issues, and did harm on others. The negatives were, in part, due to very stiff right-wing Republican opposition, divisions within the Democratic Party, weaknesses with Obama and some of his strategies, and political confusion among a large section of the American people. But, the alternative was Mitt Romney, an anti-worker corporate billionaire, who if elected would have made things considerably worse. The Romney/Ryan ticket was intent on making much deeper cuts to social services and jobs, rolling back health care reform, ratcheting up the attack on unions and the working class along with people of color and women, plunging more workers and their communities into economic crisis and poverty, threatening new wars of imperialist aggression, worsening climate change, and enriching millionaires and billionaires at the expense of the 99%.

In the 2012 elections, union members set records for the massive amount of precinct-walking, phone-banking, educational work and other voter-outreach they did all over the country for Obama and many other

Democratic Party candidates. These union members learned important organizing skills in the process. While many union activists had previous experience doing this kind of organizing, many were new to it. What is important is that all of them learned or enhanced skills that are transferrable to other work in their unions, on their jobs, in their local communities, and for larger political campaigns and movements.

Nationwide, 400,000 union volunteers, their families and allies knocked on 14 million doors, made 80 million phone calls, and registered 450,000 new voters during the 2012 election campaign, according to the AFL-CIO. The Obama/Democratic Party campaign reported that it made over 125 million phone calls or visits, reaching 1 of every 2.5 people in the country, to Romney's reported 50 million voter contacts. If these figures are accurate, union members made the lion's share of direct contacts with Obama voters. It paid off.

Among union members, 65% voted for Obama, well above the 51% of the total vote received by Obama. Among union households, counting family members, 58% voted for Obama, 7% points above the national average. With over 13 million union members, and an estimated 30-40 million voters in union households, labor delivered a tremendous vote for Obama.

Workers Were Key in 2012

In key battle-ground or "swing" states, labor ensured Obama's victory. The AFL-CIO reported that in the last four days before the election, union members, their families and their allies contacted 800,000 voters in Ohio alone. Union members make up 13.4% of Ohio's population, but 22% of all votes cast in Ohio were from union households. Obama won Ohio 50.7% to 47.7%.

Richard Trumka, president of the AFL-CIO, said in a press conference the day after the election that labor brought Obama victories in Ohio, Wisconsin and Nevada. Each of those states has a significant labor union membership. "Without organized labor," Trumka said, "none of those states would have been in the president's column." In two other battle-ground states where labor is strong, Pennsylvania and Michigan, labor played a big role in Obama victories. If Obama had lost those five states, Romney would be president today. Labor is by far the largest and most influential independent organization in the country fighting for the vast majority of the American people.

Labor has and should continue to convey to President Obama the message that his Administration must do everything possible to help unions grow and get stronger. If this doesn't happen, current trends show that unions will be weaker by the next major elections in 2014 and 2016, and battleground states and national elections will be lost to anti-labor, right-wing, Republican candidates.

In many statewide ballot initiatives, labor's role was also key and most union-backed initiatives went for labor. In California, labor and its allies, including the Democratic Party, went all out to defeat Proposition 32, a measure aimed at crippling unions' ability to participate in election campaigns by prohibiting "deductions" from worker's paychecks for political campaigns, meaning specifically union dues. The "No on 32" campaign won 56.6% to 43.4%. I worked hard on the "NO on 32" campaign, and every night that I went to the International Brotherhood of Electrical Workers (IBEW) local union hall near my house, the phone-banks were full – mostly with rank-and-file IBEW electricians. That was going on in union halls, and Democratic Party offices, all over the state.

This same labor-community-Democratic Party coalition helped pass Proposition 30, which prevented $6 billion in further cuts to education in California by raising the income tax rate on the top income earners and increasing the state sales tax by ¼ percent. Union members also worked in three cities to raise the minimum wage, San Jose, and Long Beach, California, and Albuquerque, New Mexico. In Illinois, union members were active in a successful campaign to stop an attack on workers' pensions. In Michigan, union activists helped voters reject an undemocratic law that had allowed the state to take over cities and towns suffering economic crisis from being plundered by capital, and arbitrarily remove elected officials. The cities targeted for these undemocratic take-overs have been led by African-American elected officials, casting a sharp racist edge to the assault.

Building Stewards Councils

But, labor must get stronger and build on what it did in the elections. AFL-CIO leader Trumka has recognized this need. One way to strengthen workers, especially at the work place, is to build Stewards Councils there. When workers gain economic and political strength at work, all other campaigns for improvements become easier.

A Stewards Council is an organized body of workers on the job who are union departmental stewards, and who meet regularly and work together to help each other and their co-workers. The strongest Stewards Councils have a deeply democratic internal structure and life that empowers the stewards, and the stewards, in turn, help empower their co-workers. While Stewards Councils primarily exist at unionized workplaces, they can be built in non-union workplaces as well, and even in local communities.

I began in the labor movement in 1968 while employed as union auto parts worker at Standard Mirror Company in Buffalo. We made rear-view mirrors for all Ford and Chrysler cars and trucks in the US. Our local union, organized during the CIO organizing drive of the late 1930s and early 1940s, had in its leadership workers who were members of the Communist Party. When I began to work there, the teachings of our founders were still evident. We had stewards in every department, and they helped provide leadership to the rest of us. Our local union meetings were run, in part, like a Stewards Council. We had reports from various departments, and discussion by everyone about how to deal with each department's problems. We defeated job speed-up in the department I worked in by organizing a shop floor slow-down campaign. I've worked on other jobs where we had a union but with a weak internal union structure, where stewards primarily worked alone filing grievances. The differences between these two types of situations were like the difference between day and night.

In 1998, I was working as a full-time union representative for Service Employees International Union, Local 660, in Los Angeles. My first major assignment was at Harbor-UCLA Medical Center, an LA County facility in Torrance, CA, in Los Angeles County. Within my first week, I was inundated with phone calls from members complaining about problems they said weren't being resolved. I knew there was no way that I and the five stewards there could handle the 15 complaints I was receiving every day at a medical complex with 1,700 workers. We needed to build a Stewards Council.

Worker Empowerment is Key

I asked the stewards there if they wanted to meet to discuss the problems. Three agreed, and we met at a restaurant near the hospital after work. I asked them to list all the problems, and what they had done to try to solve them. They produced a long list, and other than filing grievances, they didn't know what else to do. They felt overwhelmed. After some discussion, they understood that the four of us could not tackle all of the problems, so we had to prioritize and break them down into something more manageable. We also needed other workers to help.

We decided that we would focus on a problem that affected a group of 20-30 workers, rather than just one worker. That would strengthen our efforts, and make the workers feel that they had some ownership in the union – that they were the union. We set three criteria for choosing a group problem. (1) There had to be a problem that affected most of the workers in the work area. (2) It needed to be a problem that the workers felt strongly about. (3) There had to be a leader or potential leader in the work group.

The four of us met every week and we soon invited other interested and trusted workers to attend. Everyone participated in the discussions and decision-making. I knew that if they were involved in the process they would feel they had a real stake in what we were creating; that was important. We would be that much more effective.

Once we found a work group that met the criteria, our goals for the campaign were: (A) Involve a majority of the workers in the campaign, (B) Try to win a victory, and (C) Recruit at least one campaign leader to become a steward. Then we would repeat this process in another work area that met these criteria. Our long-term goal was to have at least one steward in every department, on every shift, in a ratio of one steward for every 20 workers. Later, we reduced that ratio to one steward for every 15 or even 10 workers.

 When we had recruited 12 stewards who were representative of the workforce, including different departments and job classifications, ethnic make-up, men and women, and young and older workers, we would set up an interim Stewards Council. When we had 20 stewards, we would establish the permanent Stewards Council.

The Council would function as a democratic body. Stewards would elect officers – president, vice president, and secretary - and write and approve a simple constitution, bylaws, and mission statement that mandated democratic practices, and encouraged member input. All the while, we would keep recruiting stewards.

Building a Campaign

We received a call from two workers on the hospital's "4 West" ward who complained that management had issued a memo stating that workers had to bring in a doctor's note if they were off one day sick in December. The usual policy had required a doctor's note after three days off. I went with one of the stewards to meet with the workers. We asked if everyone was strongly opposed to this change, and they said "yes." We decided that a petition could gauge the level of support, while assessing and teaching the petition circulators leadership skills.

Within three days, 23 of 25 workers signed the petition. We then developed a campaign with the callers. We would file a group grievance and have as many people come to the grievance meeting as possible. The lead workers mapped their work area by making a list of all the workers there, and got 12 workers to agree to come and speak at the grievance meeting. We could only get two workers released for the meeting, so the others came in on their breaks, two at a time, every 15 minutes, spread over an hour and a half. Work slowed down considerably. Management was worried, and backed off on enforcing the new rule. Workers were happy, and one leader became a steward.

We repeated this process in other work areas and within four months we formed the interim Stewards Council. Within eight months, we had built a permanent Stewards Council that elected its officers.

The council put out letters and leaflets in its name, conducted larger campaigns at the facility, and was soon seen by workers and management as the union at the work site. I worked most closely with the elected leaders of the council and together, we developed ideas for plans and campaigns to bring to the Stewards Council for discussion and a decision.

Early in the process we held steward training classes right after work at the hospital, once a week, to make it easy for stewards to attend. Topics included, "Understanding Your Contract," "Rights and Responsibilities of Stewards," "Communication and Informal Problem Solving," and "Organizing Around Worksite Issues." Most of the classes emphasized looking for group issues. I involved the stewards in the classes as much as possible, including as presenters when they felt comfortable. We repeated these classes as we got new stewards.

Developing Leaders

We also set up a mentoring program. New stewards would go with more experienced stewards or with me to meetings with management to see first-hand how issues were handled. As they gained knowledge, skills, and confidence, they began to participate more and more. Our goal was to get as many stewards as possible to run meetings with co-workers and management by themselves. This gave the union a big boost. We also publicized our activities, especially our victories.

Soon, word was out that the union was alive and growing. Workers in other areas came to us, asking to become stewards. We asked them to help on a project, and then gave them the stewards' petition to get signed by a majority of workers in their work area, making them a steward. Within a year and a half, we had 35 stewards and the union was winning some victories. Things were not perfect, but management knew the union was there.

At each Stewards Council meeting, stewards would give reports on issues or problems taking place in their department. If any steward needed help, the entire Council would discuss that department's problem and help the steward with ideas to resolve them. The steward would then go back to his or her department and work with co-workers to find a resolution. If the problem persisted, it would be brought back to the Council for more discussion and action.

After several nurse stewards reported at two Steward Council meetings that the nursing department management was still dragging its feet on scheduling grievances, the Council discussed the problem. It was decided that as many members of the Council as possible would go with the nurse stewards on a designated day to confront nursing management. We set the date a couple of weeks away so stewards could re-schedule their lunch breaks so they could participate. On the appointed day, at 12 noon, 10 stewards from different job classifications and different departments all over the hospital went on their lunch break with several nurse stewards to the nursing administration office. I joined them.

Winning Victories

When we entered the office a nursing administrator was stunned by the surprise visit and the size of the group. We clogged up the entire front office. We explained that each person there was a steward for his or her department, collectively representing several hundred workers. One after another, the stewards told the nursing administrator that it was unacceptable that the nurses' grievances weren't being heard in a timely fashion. We asked her to get out her calendar so we could schedule them right then. She was so shaken she complied. When we finished, we went down the hall to see the vice president of the medical center to lodge our complaints there, not only the nurses' problems, but other lingering problems throughout the facility. He met with us for 45 minutes, and made commitments with deadlines to move to correct the problems we raised. Early in the meeting we asked him to call each steward's department to tell management that the steward was meeting with him, in case the meeting ran past the lunch-break. He did.

Since this was the first time workers had done something this bold, management was taken back. But, it let them know that a group of workers who were worksite union leaders were serious and determined to get problems corrected. The stewards agreed that they would try to resolve the problems in their own department first. But, if that didn't work, the Stewards Council would organize a group action. For each new group action, we tried to add something. For one, the big group went to management, but took a petition signed by hundreds of workers. The message we wanted management to get was that a lot of workers were upset about unresolved problems. No one in management wanted to see their jobs and the work of their institution disrupted.

The Stewards Councils at this and other LA County facilities took on bigger issues. They, and the entire union, played a big role in helping pass "Measure B" on November 2, 2002 which generated enough money to save the Trauma Network in Los Angeles County from imminent collapse due to proposed budget cuts. This saved countless lives, and our county workers' jobs.

I was re-assigned to LAC+USC Medical Center near downtown Los Angeles, which had more than 3,500 workers. There was already a Stewards Council there of about 40 stewards and we enlarged it to over 80. We had issue campaigns going on continuously, and won many big victories, including protecting patient safety by reducing patient loads for nurses, resolving health and safety problems, reining in abusive managers, and more. The Stewards Council put out a monthly newsletter reporting on union victories and urging support for current campaigns. Stewards Councils can be organized in non-union work places as well, beginning by organizing secretly to protect the activists. When workers have a good Stewards Council, they feel that they are the union, and that they have power. And they do. They are also better equipped to work on other, even larger issues, on the job and in the community, and in election campaigns -- including running union workers for political office.

Paul Krehbiel has been an elected union steward and local union president, and has helped organize Stewards Councils at various work sites. He was the chief union negotiator for 5,000 SEIU Registered Nurses in Los Angeles, and is a member of CCDS

Let's Stop Making Migration a Crime

David Bacon argues that instead of immigration reform that includes guest worker programs and more enforcement, we need to change the free trade programs that cause migration and stop making it a crime for the undocumented to work.

By David Bacon
Via Truthout, Feb 15, 2013

A scene from the million-person march in Los Angeles in 2006. (Photo: David Bacon)

We need an immigration policy based on human, civil and labor rights, which looks at the reasons why people come to the US, and how we can end the criminalization of their status and work. While proposals from Congress and the administration have started the debate over the need for change in our immigration policy, they are not only too limited and ignore the global nature of migration, they actually will make the problem of criminalization much worse. We need a better alternative.

This alternative should start by looking at the roots of migration - the reasons why people come to the US in the first place. Movement and migration is a human right. But we live in a world in which a lot of migration isn't voluntary, but is forced by poverty and so-called economic reforms.

Our trade policy and the economic measures we impose on countries like Mexico, El Salvador or the Philippines make poverty worse. When people get poorer and their wages go down, it creates opportunities for US corporate investment. This is what drives our trade policy. But the human cost is very high.

Trade Agreements in El Salvador

In El Salvador today, the US Embassy is telling the government to sell off its water, hospitals, schools and highways to give US investors a chance to make money. This policy is enabled by the Central American Free Trade Agreement (CAFTA), whose purpose was increasing opportunities in El Salvador for US investors. It was imposed on the people of that country in the face of fierce popular opposition.

Alex Gomez, a leader of Salvadoran public-sector unions, came to San Francisco in February to explain what the consequences of this latest free trade initiative will be. He says if these public resources are privatized, tens of thousands of workers will lose their jobs, and their unions will be destroyed. They will then have to leave the country to survive.

According to Gomez, four million have already left El Salvador. Two million have come to the US, not because they love it here, but because they can't survive any longer at home. These migrants come without papers, because there are no visas for two million people from this small country.

The North American Free Trade Agreement (NAFTA) did even more damage than CAFTA. It let US corporations dump corn in Mexico, to take over the market there with imports from the US. Today one company, Smithfield Foods, sells almost a third of all the pork consumed by Mexicans. Because of this dumping and the market takeover, prices dropped so low that millions of Mexican farmers couldn't survive. They too had to leave home.

Mexico used to be self-sufficient in corn and meat production. Corn cultivation started there in Oaxaca many centuries ago. Now Mexico is a net corn and meat importer from the US.

During the years NAFTA has been in effect, the number of Mexican-born people in the US went from 4.5 million to 12.67 million. Today about 11 percent of all Mexicans live in the US. About 5.7 million of those who came were able to get some kind of visa, but another 7 million couldn't. There just aren't that many visas. But they came anyway because they had very little choice, if they wanted to survive or their families to prosper.

Our immigration laws turn these people into criminals. They say that if migrants without papers work here it's a crime. But how can people survive here if they don't work? We need a different kind of immigration policy - one that stops putting such pressure on people to leave, and that doesn't treat them as criminals if they do.

What would it look like?

First, we should tell the truth, as the TRADE Act, introduced into Congress by Rep. Mike Michaud (D-Maine), would have us do. We should hold hearings as the bill says, about the effects of NAFTA and CAFTA, and collect evidence about the way those agreements have displaced people in the US and other countries as well.

Then we need to renegotiate those existing agreements to eliminate the causes of displacement. If we provide compensation to communities that have suffered the effects of free trade and corporate economic reforms that were intended to benefit US investors, it would be more than simple justice. It might give people more resources and more of a future at home.

It makes no sense to negotiate new trade agreements that displace even more people or lower living standards. This administration has negotiated three so far - with Peru, Panama and South Korea. It is now negotiating a new one - the Trans Pacific Partnership. These are all pro-corporate, people-displacing agreements. We should prohibit these and any new ones like them. Instead, we need to make sure all future trade treaties require adequate farm prices and income in farming communities, promote unions and high wages and don't require the privatization of public services.

Increasingly these international agreements, like Mode 4 of the World Trade Organization, treat displaced migrants as a cheap and vulnerable labor force. Our trade negotiators call for regulating their flow with guest worker programs. This is exactly the wrong direction. We should instead ban the inclusion of guest workers in any future trade agreement or treaty.

When diplomacy doesn't work, US military intervention and aid programs are to support trade agreements, structural adjustment policies or market economic reforms. This has been US policy in Honduras and Haiti, for instance. This also must stop. If the US Embassy is putting pressure on countries like El Salvador to adopt measures that benefit corporate investors at the expense of workers and farmers, the Ambassador should be recalled and the interference halted.

Finally, we should ratify the UN Convention on the Rights of Migrant Workers and Their Families. This international agreement would give us an alternative framework for recognizing the rights of displaced migrants, and the responsibility of both sending and receiving countries for their protection.

The failure of successive US administrations to even present this agreement to Congress for ratification highlights the unpleasant truth about the real effect of our immigration policy. When millions of migrants arrive here, they are criminalized because they lack immigration status, especially when they go to work.

Migrant and civil rights advocates often fondly remember the 1986 Immigration Reform and Control Act because it had an amnesty, signed by President Ronald Reagan, which gave legal status relatively quickly to almost four million people. But the law also contained employer sanctions for the first time, which we often forget. That provision says that employers will be fined and punished if they hire undocumented workers. This provision was promoted by those who said that if work became illegal, then undocumented migration would end. This clearly failed, since the number increased many fold in the years that followed. Compared to the pressure to leave home, criminalizing work was not a deterrent to those who sought work here so that their families at home would survive.

This provision sounded like a law against employers, but it was not. It became an anti-worker law. No boss ever went to jail for violating it. The fines were not great. When the government agents seek to enforce it, employers who cooperate with them are forgiven. But over the last four years alone, tens of thousands of workers have been fired for not having papers. The true objects of punishment under this law have always been workers, not employers.

Now Congress is talking about a new reform, and we have to use this opportunity to push to repeal this law. Some think that since a new legalization hopefully will give many undocumented workers legal status, sanctions won't really affect anyone anymore.

But even the most positive predictions about a new legalization still assume that millions of people will not qualify because of stringent qualifications, high fees and decades-long waiting periods. Those people still will be subject to the sanctions law. And the day after a new reform passes, millions more people will come to the US because of the same pressures that caused past waves of migration. This is especially true if a new immigration reform ignores the need to renegotiate trade agreements and eliminate the huge displacement of people.

These future migrants are not strangers. They are the husbands and wives, parents and cousins of people already here - people who are already part of our communities. They come from the same towns, and are linked to neighborhoods here in the US by the ties that have been created by migration, work and family. We need to keep the sanctions law from being applied to them, making it a crime for them to work. Unfortunately, however, members of Congress aren't talking about getting rid of sanctions. In fact, they and the administration want to make the current application even worse.

So let's do a reality check. Let's tell the truth about how this law has been used.

One method for enforcing sanctions happens when employers use an error-riddled government database called E-verify to screen people they plan to hire. Congress and the administration are calling to make it mandatory for all employers to use this database, and to refuse to hire anyone it flags as undocumented.

For people who are currently working now and have no papers, this means if they lose their jobs, it will be much harder to find a new one. That will make people fear taking any action that offends their boss, like joining a union or complaining about illegal conditions. That's good for the boss, but bad for the workers.

Employers today not only use this database to screen new hires - they also use it to re-verify the immigration status of people who are already working. This is a violation of the law. Once employers accept the form filled out by a job seeker (called the I-9), along with their ID, they can't re-verify it all over again at some point in the future. But they do. Sometimes it's convenient to get rid of workers who have accumulated benefits and raises over years of service, and replace them with new hires at lower wages.

Re-verification just happened, for instance, to three workers who belong to the International Longshore and Warehouse Union at Waste Management Inc. in San Leandro, California. The union has gone to the Oakland City Council to protest these illegal firings, because WMI operates under a city garbage contract.

Employers sometimes announce they intend to begin using the E-Verify database when their workers start to organize. That's what managers announced at the Mi Pueblo supermarkets in northern California. E-Verify checks are being used there to terrorize workers to keep them from supporting Local 5 of the United Food and Commercial Workers Union. Another method for enforcing sanctions against workers is even more widespread. Immigration agents, working for US Immigration and Customs Enforcement (ICE), go into the personnel records of an employer. They then compare the information given by workers on the I-9 form to the E-Verify database, looking for workers who don't have legal immigration status. ICE then makes a list of those workers and sends it to the company, telling the employer to fire them.

This is what happened at Pacific Steel Castings in Berkeley, California, last year. Two hundred and fourteen workers were fired as a result. Some had worked in the foundry for more than 20 years. Many lost their homes, and their children's dreams of going to college were destroyed. Hundreds of thousands of workers have lost their jobs in these enforcement actions, called I-9 audits, over last four years, including almost 500 janitors in San Francisco, and more than a thousand in Minneapolis. Thousands of workers doing some of the hardest work imaginable in meatpacking plants around the country. Farm workers. Construction workers. But the employers are all given reduced fines, and many received immunity from punishment entirely if they cooperated in firing their own workers.

Resistance is Possible

If unions and communities mount a fight that exposes the terrible human cost of these firings, it is possible to stop them. The young Dreamers showed that this is possible. These courageous young people convinced the administration to stop deporting students brought to the US without papers as children. They forced the administration to change the way it enforces immigration law. It can be done for workers too, if there's a fight.

But we must also change the sanctions law. Otherwise, our experience over the 25 years since it passed shows that immigration authorities will simply find another method to make working a crime for people who don't have papers.

The other unpleasant truth about sanctions is that they are linked to the growth of guest worker programs. One of the main purposes of making it a crime to work without papers is to force people to come to the US with visas that tie them to their employers and recruiters. These workers are often more vulnerable than the undocumented, since they get deported if they lose their jobs or get fired. Guest worker programs have been called Close to Slavery by the Southern Poverty Law Center and others who have documented their extreme exploitation. The sanctions law functions as a way to pressure people into choosing that path to come to the US to work.

When employer sanctions are used to make workers vulnerable to pressure, to break unions or to force people into guest worker programs, their real effect is to force people into low wage jobs with no rights. This is a subsidy for employers, and brings down wages for everyone. The sanctions law makes it harder for all workers to organize to improve conditions. This doesn't just affect the workers who have no papers themselves. When it becomes harder for one group to organize, other workers have a harder time organizing too.

Some Washington insiders accept as a fact of life that the sanctions law will continue, or even worse, that E-Verify will become a mandatory national program for all employers. But for unions and workers who have had to deal with its effects, it would be much better to immediately repeal it, and dismantle the E-Verify database. This in fact was the decision taken by the AFL-CIO at its convention in Los Angeles in 1999. Delegates at that convention believed we have to stop enforcing immigration law in the workplace, because its real effect is to make workers vulnerable to employers, and to make it harder for all workers to organize to improve conditions.

In addition to repealing the national sanctions law, we should also prohibit states from enacting copycat measures. These laws have passed not just in Arizona or Alabama or Mississippi. California passed a state employer sanctions law before the federal law took effect in 1986.

What would really help workers to raise wages and improve conditions is much stricter enforcement of worker protection and anti-discrimination laws - for everyone. Funding used for immigration enforcement on the job should be given instead to the Department of Labor, the Occupational Safety and Health Administration, the National Labor Relations Board and other labor law enforcement agencies. It will be a good day for all workers when ICE agents instead become wage and hour inspectors.

Threats by employers who use immigration status to keep workers from organizing unions or protesting illegal conditions should be a crime. That makes it necessary to overturn two Supreme Court decisions, Hoffman and Sure-Tan. In these cases the court said that if workers are fired for union activity and have no papers, the boss doesn't have to rehire them or pay them lost wages, because the sanctions law makes it illegal to employ them to begin with. But when there's no punishment for violating labor rights, workers have no rights. This also hurts other workers in the same workplace who want to organize a union, since it makes the undocumented so vulnerable. Instead, we should increase workplace rights by prohibiting immigration enforcement during labor disputes or against workers who complain about illegal conditions.

Social Security as Ripoff

To ensure that in the workplace we all have the same rights, we also have to eliminate the way undocumented people get ripped off by funds like Social Security and unemployment. All workers contribute to the Social Security fund, but because undocumented people are working under bad numbers, they pay in but can never collect the benefits. This will come back to haunt us when those workers need disability payments or get too old to work - something that happens to us all. This is the reason we set up the Social Security system to begin with - because we don't want old people eating dog food, regardless of where they were born.

Instead today the Social Security number has become much more a means to check immigration status, harming workers instead of providing them the benefits that were its original and true purpose. There is a simple solution to this problem as well. Social Security numbers should be made available for everyone, regardless of immigration status. Everyone should pay into the system and everyone has a right to the benefits those payments create. By the same token all workers should be able to receive unemployment benefits regardless of status, since they and their employers pay into the funds.

In the end, we need an immigration policy that brings people together, instead of pitting workers against each other, as our current system does. During a time of economic crisis especially, we need to reduce job competition, rather than stoking fears. In 2005 Congresswoman Sheila Jackson Lee of Houston made an innovative proposal that would have set up job creation and training programs for unemployed workers at the same time that it would have given legal status to workers without papers. This proposal put unemployed workers and immigrants on the same side, giving them both something to fight for whether they were out of work, or working without immigration status. This proposal, and the others made here, are all part of the Dignity Campaign, a plan for immigration reform based on human, civil and labor rights.

An immigration policy that benefits migrants, their home communities, and working people here in the US has to have a long-term perspective. Instead of just trying to please interest groups well-represented in Congress, we need to ask, where are we going? What will actually solve the problems that we experience with current laws and policies?

We need a system that produces security, not insecurity. We need a commitment to equality and equal status - getting rid of color and national lines instead of making them deeper. We need to make it easier for workers to organize, by getting rid of what makes people vulnerable - to end job competition we need full employment, and to gain organizing rights we need labor law enforcement together with eliminating sanctions and firings. It's not likely that many corporations will support such a program, so the politicians who represent us have to choose whose side they're on.

Working people in Mexico, El Salvador, the Philippines, the US and other countries need the same things. Secure jobs at a living wage. Rights in our workplaces and communities. The freedom to travel and seek a future for our families, and the ability to stay home and have a decent future there, too. The borders between our countries, then, should be common grounds that unite us, not lines that divide us.

David Bacon is a writer and photographer. His new book, Illegal People - How Globalization Creates Migration and Criminalizes Immigrants, was just published by Beacon Press. His photographs and stories can be found at http://dbacon.igc.org.

Ray Elizondo and 'The Last Pachuco': An Interview with the Chicano Writer Conducted by Paul Krehbiel

"From the barrios of Brownsville, Texas, springs this tale of defiance and daring. Ray Elizondo, a young Pachuco, bashed the skull of an attacker with a metal pipe at a high school football game and his life was changed forever."

-From the back cover of The Last Pachuco, by Ray Elizondo

D&I: When did you first become aware of the Pachucos?

Elizondo: When I was five years old. It was 1942. I was coming home from the gas station a block away from where we lived with kerosene for my mother. We used kerosene to light our stove. As I neared a local cantina, I heard yelling and fighting, and saw a man stumble down the stairs, holding part of his brain in his hand. He collapsed on a bench and died. I was five feet from him and terrified. The police came and asked the crowd, "who did this?" Someone said "a damn Pachuco." So, I saw Pachucos as dangerous men at that young age.

D&I: That was a terrible experience. As you got older, did you change your view of Pachuco's?

Elizondo: Yes. When I saw some older Pachucos in our neighborhood stand up for themselves when they were attacked by another group for no reason. The Pachucos were out-numbered, but they fought back and defended themselves. So, I sympathized with them. They were about 14 or 15 years old. I was about 7.

D&I: How would you describe the Pachucos?

Elizondo: They were proud. They were proud of their Mexican-American heritage, and demanded to be treated with respect. We created our own

culture. We dressed sharp, with our tailored cuffed pants, and our bo-
lero style shirts that fit tight and puffed out in the sleeves. And we wore
double soled Stacey Adam shoes, when we could afford them. Those
shoes had a little larger heel, and the toes tipped up in the front. We
were seen as rebels. Mainstream society shunned us, but a lot of girls
were attracted to us. We were all young, in our teens and twenties.

D&I: Were the Pachucos political?

Elizondo: Not in the sense that most people think of when they think of
politics, or political activity. But, the fact that the Pachucos stood tall and
said, "We're here, we're going to be recognized, and respected," was important. Many people say that the Pachucos helped lay the ground for the
Chicano movement of the 1960s. You have to remember that we came
along at a time when Mexican-Americans were treated as second-class
citizens in our own country. We were expected to be passive, go along
with whoever was in charge, keep our heads down, don't make waves,
know our place in society, which was as farm laborers, factory workers,
maids, and the like. Mexican-Americans were 70% of the population of
Brownsville. The whites owned most of the businesses, and the Mexican-
Americans worked for them. Most business owners lived well, especially
by our standards, and the majority of Mexican-Americans were poor.

D&I: Were there other signs of opposition to this second-class
citizen status?

Elizondo: There were strikes by the workers in the seaport. Maybe some
other protests, but not much that I was aware of.

D&I: Can you tell us what it was like growing up in your family?

Elizondo: I was the youngest of four children. My parents were from
Mexico, but my brother, two sisters and I were born in Brownsville. My
dad died when I was four, and my older brother was already grown and
out of the house. So, my mom, two sisters and I lived in a poor barrio.
My mom took in laundry and washed it in big tubs in the yard, and did
ironing to survive. One of my sisters quit school when she was 9 to help
my mom with this work. My other sister and I helped out when we could.
That sister got married at age 15 and left the house, so then it was just
the three of us.

D&I: Please tell us about your memoir, The Last Pachuco

Elizondo: It's a coming-of-age story set in Brownsville. It's about the
adventures of a young man trying to find his identity in the middle of

the 20th century, and the important role the Pachuco movement played in that, and the turmoil, love, tragedy, and finally redemption that he experiences.

D&I: You were sent to the most notorious reform school in Texas at age 15 after the fight at a high school football game. Can you talk about that?

Elizondo: It was a learning experience. I learned something about inner strength there. Here's one example. I was assigned to work in the kitchen, 7 days a week. I didn't think it was right to have to work every day without a day off, so I refused to work and went on a hunger strike. They threw me in solitary confinement. I spent the time counting all the rivets in my cell, in total darkness. They thought they could break me, but they didn't. Eventually, I won. There were other traumatic experiences there, but I don't want to tell them and ruin it for those who want to read the book.

D&I: When did you get interested in writing?

Elizondo: When I got out of solitary confinement, I began reading a lot of books. That started my interest in literature. Many years later, in the early 1980's, I was working for a Chicano rights group in Los Angeles that was trying to help Chicano's find jobs. We worked with a group of young Chicano actors, writers and directors, and organized picket-lines in front of theaters on Sunset Blvd. in Hollywood for not hiring Chicano artists. Some of the people involved were James Edward Olmos – the famous actor, Frank Zuniga – a film director, and Montezuma Esbarta – an actor and director. After our protests, some Chicano artists got more work. This got me interested in writing. I was busy with my job and family so I had limited time to write, but I found time. I took some courses at several universities, and later joined writers groups. I've written five manuscripts. The Last Pachuco is my first published one.

Ray Elizondo is a former semi-professional boxer, paratrooper, construction worker, and an award-winning hair stylist. The Last Pachuco is available at autumnleafpress.com, in paperback for $14.95, plus shipping

Juicing Up the Labor Movement? - Try Speaking to 'Women's Issues'

By Linda Gordon

This was originally published by In These Times, January 21, 2013 as "Why Abortion is a Labor Issue. Can unions team with feminists to create an 'American Spring'." Reprinted with permission of the author.

On December 11, 2012 the state of Michigan passed two right-to-work laws, one for public and one for private employees. As even our president said, they mean right to work for lower wages. These laws do not make workers free to reject joining a union; they already have that right. They abolish the requirement that those who don't join a union pay the equivalent of union dues, a requirement designed to prevent "free riders" - workers who benefit from union contracts without paying their fair share. Three days later the same lame-duck legislature passed the most extreme anti-abortion laws in the nation. These laws define as abortion even the removal of a "fetus that has died as a result of natural causes, accidental trauma, or a criminal assault on the pregnant woman." The laws prohibit any private or public insurance from covering abortion; charge physicians performing abortion with the responsibility of seeing that any piece of human tissue receive the burial due to a deceased person; put the burden on the physician to prove that the abortion patient was not coerced. Perhaps worst, the laws place many arbitrary requirements on clinics, none of them health related, and would force most of the state's women's clinics to close.

This coincidence of anti-labor and anti-abortion legislation is not a coincidence. They are part of the same right-wing agenda. If progressives are to build successful resistance to that agenda, our own agenda needs to include both labor and reproductive rights.

But unions and other supporters of labor have ignored reproductive rights. Some of this hands-off position came from deference to Catholics, but if that was once reasonable, it no longer is. Over 95 percent of Catholics use contraception in defiance of the church's teaching and plenty of Catholics have abortions. Another reason for ignoring reproductive rights was the traditional maleness of unions, also no longer the case.

But the worst problem has been defining reproductive rights as a "women's issue" and a feminist demand, which evokes the old labor and Left view that feminism is a movement of elites. That's wrong too: if you ask women not about the label "feminism," but about the issues that make up a feminist program - such as equal pay, equal job opportunity, affordable day care, shared housework, an end to violence against women, and reproductive rights - it turns out that working-class and poor women are the most feminist.

'War on Women' Targets Us All

In fact, the Republican "war on women" is not just targeting women, any more than the war on labor is targeting only men. All middle- and working-class people, and especially the poor, benefit from a strong labor movement -it's our best bulwark against a race to the wage bottom. In parallel, being able to control how many children to have and when to have them is something men as well as women need. Access to birth control has become a necessity of modern life, and this is the opinion of the majority of Americans of all groups, including African Americans, Latino Americans, and Muslim Americans.

The great majority of abortion decisions are made jointly by the men and women responsible for the pregnancy. The great majority of abortion decisions rest on economic considerations: we can't afford a child, or another child; we can't survive on one income; child care is too expensive for us; it would be better to finish high school, or college, or graduate school first; it's too soon after the previous birth; I can no longer rely on my mother or sister or grandmother for help.

In other words, anti-abortion laws amount to class legislation, even if not all their proponents realize that. As in the past, during the century when abortion was made illegal, the well-to-do always found ways to obtain abortions through paying private physicians or traveling to countries more realistic about sex and the economy. It's working-class and middle-class people and the young who depend on the clinics that the Michigan law will close. One-quarter of all poor women who get birth control get it at one of these family planning clinics and for many, they are the first entry point into any adult health care. At most clinics, initial visits are free and fees for further services depend on income - for the poor, typically $20. The majority of clinics provide women with post-partum and prenatal care, well-baby care, immunizations, and physical exams. More than 40 percent provide primary health care and many also provide genetic screening, mammograms, infertility counseling and mental health care.

These clinics are usually the only source of reproductive health care for the most marginalized groups: drug abusers, prison inmates, the disabled and the homeless. And they often serve men as well as women, providing HIV testing and referrals, safe sex instruction, and prostate and testicular cancer screening.

Other abortion decisions are made by teenagers who don't have access to contraception, or whose partners pressure them into sex and won't use condoms, or who think that using contraception makes them "sluts." These are the women who are least well prepared to be parents at the time.

The best way to reduce abortions is of course to make contraception easily accessible and free. (Although most anti- abortion advocates also oppose these measures.) But accidents happen; contraception is not flawless. And neither are people. Sex is an unruly force. That's why, as all teenagers know, abstinence education doesn't work.

Resistance and Growing Awareness

But there's an immediate political consideration too: however misnamed, the "war on women" angered and mobilized women across class lines. The Republican attacks elicited an outpouring of money and support for Planned Parenthood; when the Komen breast-cancer foundation tried to cut off support for Planned Parenthood, it was forced to take back its threat within days. This resistance represents a growing awareness of the dangers of the right-wing agenda. Pro-choice people tend to be progressive on many other issues too, including domestic spending and foreign policy. But not all understand fully how destroying labor unions pushes everyone's standard of living downward.

Here in Wisconsin the massive uprising against the Scott Walker/ALEC agenda in 2011 was probably majority female. Then in his victorious election campaign, Walker appealed explicitly to his base of white men, talking up hunting, guns, and projecting a combative, aggressive image, while the anti- Walker campaign noticeably neglected raising any of the "women's issues." Instead, the anti-Walker forces should have prioritized the connections between his anti-union and anti- women's rights agenda. Union forces simply can't afford to write off "women's issues" as outside their concern. Building an alliance between feminist groups and the labor movement should be a high priority.

Linda Gordon was born in Chicago but considers Portland, Oregon, her home town. She went to college at Swarthmore then received her Ph.D. from Yale in Russian History in 1970. She became one of a pioneering generation of historians of the US examining women and gender. An active participant in the women's-liberation movement of the late 1960s and 1970s, she and her long-time collaborator Rosalyn Baxandall edited two books providing crucial views of that movement's contributions: America's Working Women (Random House/Vintage 1976 and 1995) and Dear Sisters: Dispatches from Women's Liberation (Basic Books, 1995).

She is a professor of history at New York University (NYU), teaching courses on gender, social movements, imperialism and the 20th-century US in general. She has won many prestigious awards, including Guggenheim, NEH, ACLS, Radcliffe Institute and the New York Public Library's Cullman Center fellowships.

Her first book, Woman's Body, Woman's Right: The History of Birth Control in America (Viking/Penguin, 1976), published in 1976 and reissued in 1990, remains the definitive history of birth-control politics in the US. It was completely revised and re-published as The Moral Property of Women in 2002.

A Letter from 'HK on J' in North Carolina to Those Who Love Justice Everywhere

Rev. Dr. William J. Barber, II
February 2013. Raleigh, NC

And a thank you to members, attendees and supporters of the Historic Thousands on Jones Street (HKonJ) People's Assembly Coalition Movement

Tuesday of this week marked the 104th birthday of the NAACP, the 204th birthday of Abraham Lincoln, and the first day of freedom for our brother, John McNeil, as he walked out of the prison system of Georgia and returned to his N.C. home – Hallelujah – my heart overflows with love for all of you.

We must never forget how far we have come in resurrecting the old Black-White-Brown Civil Rights/Labor southern movement of the 1960's and 1860's just by working together. Ordinary black and white people have been turned back twice when they set out together on the road to-ward southern fusion politics. For 33 years after Mr. Lincoln signed the Emancipation Proclamation in 1865, courageous black and white activists formed fusion political alliances and won power across the state. But in 1898, rich racists organized and funded a violent terrorist attack to crush the fusion movement, first in Wilmington, then across the South.

For 14 years after the NAACP struck down Jim Crow in 1954, creating a fertile ground for rebuilding an integrated South, another set of rich racists brainwashed violent men who bombed little girls going to Sunday school, bombed the homes of white and black civil rights activists, and assassinated our leaders, to restore the racist apartheid system that breached God's human family.

These forces pulled out, left the Democratic Party, and found a welcome mat in the new, increasingly monochromatic Republican Party. They set out to divide God's human family by race again, and once the wedges were in place, it was a simple matter to strangle these two Reconstruction movements.

A Third Reconstruction

This time . . . this time, my sisters and brothers, we will build the Third Reconstruction Movement on a strong foundation of love, mutual respect, and a burning for justice for all. We shall never be divided or defeated. On Saturday, February 9, 2013, my eyes saw all of you, thousands of black and white and brown people marching, singing, dancing, and learning. Together! What a sight! Our best estimate is that over 17,000 of us were there. Over 350 rows of about 50 people were squeezed in the two bloc plaza between the Capitol and our stage on Jones Street. That's 17,500 human beings of all ages.

We didn't even add in the large crowd on the two arms of the cross extending out on Jones Street. So we conservatively estimate 17,000. Our elders tell me it was by far the largest, most diverse, best-organized People's Assembly the NAACP has ever organized in the South. Since we began our annual people's assembly in NC, I know this was our largest and best organized.

We noted that one paper claimed on Sunday morning it was news when two white women dressed up like Latinos with big fake mustaches and ate donuts. For us, real news is when real people, dress up like themselves, bring their own real passions about making this a better world for everyone, and join with other real people, march in long rows, hundreds of rows, from the home of the Student Nonviolent Coordinating Committee (SNCC) at Shaw University to the People's House, the NC General Assembly on Jones Street. It's news when real Latinos, who hate the stereotypes of sombreros and mustaches, march with their black sisters and brothers, and their white, Asian and Native American sisters and brothers—all working toward building a fairer society for all. It's news when white, brown and black people all agree with Gen. Colin Powell's assessment of the current Republican Party that looks "down on minorities" and that has a "dark vein of intolerance" running through it.

It"s news, we believe, when thousands of people at home send their children and church members to represent them in a major assembly on Jones Street to say they know that over 51% of the voters in the past election voted against the dark vein of intolerance in the 13 congressional districts. They learned about the racist gerrymandering trick of the party that looks down on minorities, when they woke up to find that 9 out of the 13 candidates elected were Republican! Everyone knows that is not right.

Challenge to the Far Right

It's big news when the largest civil rights assembly in the history of Raleigh gathers on Jones Street to challenge the far-right's attack on the poor and working people of our state. It's big news when more college and high school students rally at the statehouse than ever before in modern history with 15 colleges sending bus loads and car-fulls of students who promise to return to their schools to organize against the policies of intolerance and racial chauvinism. It's news when twice as many immigrants participated at this Assembly than in the past, with passionate immigrant leaders speaking in Spanish and English about the growing Black-Brown-White coalition and the need for comprehensive immigration reform.

It's news when over 15 national labor leaders come from across the nation and tell us that HKonJ is the most exciting new political coalition in the country, and pledge to us they will help place more organizers in other southern states to build similar coalitions.

It's news when the largest organization of workers in NC, the widely respected North Carolina Association of Educators (NCAE), decides to join with us and place its considerable power and statewide membership in the same big tent with the thousands of NC NAACP members in 125 branches, youth councils and college chapters, along with the considerable strength of the American Association of Retired Persons (AARP), and the hundreds of thousands of members of all the church denominations who decided to become partners to resist the right-wing's attack on public education, from pre-kindergarten to graduate schools.

It's news when the NAACP and the LGBT community publicly display their political alliance and LGBT leaders vow to throw their considerable political and economic power into the fight to block the latest Republican effort to suppress our votes through a new poll tax they call "photo ID." It's news when the environmental movement joins the civil rights, labor, and peace movements, to bring their message of a sustainable economy to all of us.

It's news when half the speakers and a third of the marchers are younger than 25. High school and college students rode in the night before, slept on the floor at Martin Street Baptist, and made new friends from other schools to help build the movement against racism, poverty, and war. It's news when two of the most powerful movement leaders in the country--NAACP Chair Roslyn Brock and Dr. Ben Chavis, came to Raleigh to share our stage. We have plenty of room in this new Movement, for our elders like Dr. Chavis and our younger leaders like Ms. Brock.

I conclude by thanking each of you for your daily contributions to building the Movement, and for your hard work over the past few months in the face of a steady stream of intolerance and arrogance by our legislative leaders. I believe they heard us loud and clear: their backlash against the poor and working people of North Carolina will be resisted. The Third Reconstruction Movement is alive and well—thanks to you. We shall never go back. We will continue to build a mighty multi-racial nonviolent Movement, ready and willing to resist these attacks on the least of these.

Yours in the Struggle for Justice,

Barbarism, a Pardon and Continuing Struggle: Notes on the Historic Importance of the Wilmington Ten Case.

By Frank Chapman
NAARPR

"We have organized, participated in and will celebrate at this Conference two major victories won this past year: the release and vindication of our national co-chairperson Rev. Ben Chavis and the Wilmington Ten and George Merritt, member of our national board. While we celebrate these victories we are keenly aware of the continued attempts to stifle dissent, to silence every activist in the movements for equality, peace, freedom and solidarity with other peoples. Such dangers are represented by our government's continued prosecution of courageous peace activist David Truong. These threats are also confronted daily by our numerous organizational efforts: the fight for Johnny Imani Harris' release from death row, only miles from Birmingham; the struggle to free Native American activist Leonard Peltier; stopping the mass murder vis-a-vis the death penalty planned for the Pontiac brothers; abolishing the behavior control unit and the brutal persecution of prisoners at Marion, Illinois; and at a thousand other hell-holes from Santa Fe to Leavenworth to MacAlister, Soledad and Parchman. Our Conference will address this continuing barbarism and seek to redress it."

The above statement was taken from the Call for the Sixth National Conference of The National Alliance Against Racist and Political Repression held in Birmingham, Alabama in 1981.

Who Were the Wilmington Ten?

The Wilmington Ten were Rev. Ben Chavis, nine young men who were still in high school, and a white woman who were convicted in 1971 of arson and conspiracy. The NAARPR took the case of the Wilmington Ten up at its founding convention and subsequently launched a national and international campaign making it a cause célèbre.

How Did This Come About?

The 1970s, coming in the wake of Dr. Martin Luther King's assassination, was the beginning of what became known as the backlash against gains of the Civil Rights Movement of the 1960s. The government's response to the ghetto uprisings (then called race riots) that occurred on the evening of Dr. King's assassination and afterwards, was punitive, violent and repressive.

In 1969, just a year after the murder of Dr. King and the riots, there was an attempt to integrate the high schools of Wilmington, N.C. The city used this attempted integration as a pretext for closing Williston High School, the pride of the African American community. Black teachers and coaches were laid off and students transferred. The school administrators refused to meet with parents and students. There were no preparations for these abrupt changes. Tensions sprouted up giving rise to clashes between white and black students. There followed arrests and expulsions.

In an effort to exploit these racial tensions, the KKK and other white supremacists began patrolling the streets in an attempt to intimidate and terrorize African Americans. Consequently street violence broke out between the Klan and African American men. Also students decided to boycott the high schools. This occurred in January, 1971.

In February, 1971 the United Church of Christ sent Rev. Ben Chavis, director of their Commission for Racial Justice, to Wilmington, N.C. to ease tensions and work with students and the community for a peaceful and just solution.

Rev. Chavis advocated non-violence in the manner of the late Dr. King, and upon arriving he immediately proceeded to organize the students and the community. There were regular meetings with discussions on the history of African American freedom struggles and the need to organize a boycott.

Within a week (on Feb. 7, 1971) Mike's Grocery, a white-owned business, was allegedly fire-bombed and the responding firefighters claimed they were shot at by snipers. Rev. Chavis and the students were peacefully assembled at the church. A riot broke out in the community, lasting into the next day and claiming the lives of two people. On Feb. 8, Governor Robert Scott called out the National Guard. They forced their way into the church, alleging that they found ammunition.

By the end of the day there were two deaths, six injuries and $500,000 in property damages. Rev. Chavis, eight young African American men, who were high school students, and a white woman who was an anti-poverty worker, were arrested and charged with arson. Based on the false testimony of two black men, the Wilmington Ten were tried, convicted and sentenced to a total of 282 years. One witness said he was given a mini bike in exchange for his testimony. The other witness had a history of mental illness.

TABLE OF SENTENCES

Name Age Sentence
Rev. Ben Chavis 24 34 years
Connie Tindall 21 31 years
James "Bun" McKay 19 29 years
Wayne More 19 29 years
Melvin "Chili" Patrick 19 29 years
Reginald Epps 18 28 years
Jerry Jacobs 19 29 years
Willie Earl Vereen 18 29 years
William "Joe" Wright 19 29 years
Ann Shepard 36 15 years

Highlights of NAARPR's Campaign to Free the Wilmington Ten

The National Alliance Against Racist and Political Repression mobilized tens of thousands in protest through nationwide rallies and demonstrations in New York, Chicago, Detroit, Philadelphia, Washington, D.C., Los Angeles, Oakland, Louisville, St. Louis, Newark, Pittsburgh, and throughout the state of North Carolina culminating in a national mass demonstration in Raleigh in 1976.

From 1977-80 we collected tens of thousands of signatures on petitions to Free the Wilmington Ten directed to Governor James B. Hunt. These petitions were signed by people in the US and throughout the world. We were supported by trade union organizations, parliamentarians, supreme courts justices, writers, artists, students, people from all walks of life throughout Europe, India, China, Ethiopia, Angola, Cuba, Canada and South Africa.

In 1978 the NAARPR and the National Conference of Black Lawyers filed a petition with the United Nations Human Rights Commission charging the US government with Human Rights violations in the cases of the Wilmington Ten, Leonard Peltier, Johnny Imani Harris, Geronimo Pratt and many other political prisoners.

When President Jimmy Carter visited the Soviet Union in 1978 he was reminded by Soviet leaders of the human rights violations in the Wilmington Ten case.

In 1980, the 4th Circuit Court of Appeals, a federal court, overturned the convictions, as it determined that (1) the prosecutor failed to disclose exculpatory evidence, in violation of the defendants' due process rights [the Brady rule]; and (2) the trial judge erred by limiting the cross-examination of key prosecution witnesses about special treatment the witnesses received in connection with their testimony, in violation of the defendants' 6th Amendment right to confront the witnesses against them. Chavis v. State of North Carolina, 637 F.2d 213 (4th Cir. 1980).

A Luta Continua (The Struggle Continues)

We adopted the slogan A Luta Continua from our sisters and brothers who led the revolution in Angola against the then Portuguese colonial government. Today more than ever we need to invoke this slogan and inscribe it on our banners as we did in 1973.

The National Alliance Against Racist and Political Repression was founded in the city of Chicago 39 years ago. Our formation came in the wake of the movement to Free Angela Davis and All Political Prisoners and was truly a watershed moment in the history of the democratic struggles of the masses of our people for labor rights, human rights and peace. We also felt an urgent need to respond to the planned destruction of our movement by the FBI and CIA through their counter intelligence program known as COINTELPRO. We came about as a result of the particular need of our movement to defend itself against the racist and political repression used by the local, state and federal governments to stymie and destroy us. We came together in the light of our deep and abiding concern for the democratic rights and aspirations of the overwhelming majority of the American people. We came together because we realized that government at the local, state and federal levels was being used to contain and eliminate any and everyone challenging the status quo. Our mission was clearly to defend and extend the democratic rights of the people.

The recent pardon of the Wilmington Ten by the outgoing Governor of North Carolina is a living testament to the fact that mass, organized struggles can be victorious in the fight against racist and political repression. The NAACP played a decisive and heroic role in waging a successful campaign for the pardon of the Wilmington Ten. They delivered the final blow for justice in this case.

Today as we approach our fortieth anniversary our movement faces new dangers and historically unprecedented attacks against democracy. That is why the struggle must continue. Yesterday it was the Wilmington Ten, today its Mumia Abu Jamal, Leonard Peltier, the torture victims of Illinois and Guantanamo, and countless others who are in prison due to racist frame-ups and wrongful convictions.

The Obama Presidency and the Black Progressive

By Sharon A. Pittman

The role that Barack Obama is to play in the struggle for African American empowerment is currently the focus of heated debates among many Black progressives. Described by Louis Farrakhan as a Black man in the "White" house, Obama is regarded by many as merely a darker complexioned tool of the state that by nature of the system itself cannot deviate to any significant degree from its historically oppressive plan any more than anyone else who has held his position.

For those who did not realize this during or before his first term in office, actions such as the use of drones, his poor track record in terms of ignoring the plight of left-wing political prisoners, and his hesitancy to introduce discourse on the problems that African Americans continue to face due to race have ended many Black progressives' love affair with Obama.

The issues that tend to be the most important to Blacks in general and Black progressives in particular have to a significant degree been ignored by the Black man who sits in the White House. In some cases, those battles that he does choose to enter are approached in much the same way that a right-wing leader would, such as by increasing the military's power and decreasing the rights of citizens. For example, it is under his presidency that citizens will be denied due process in accordance with the whims of the state. He signed into law the indefinite detention provision, which is likely to be disproportionately applied to people of color.

There is a stark difference between the viewpoints that African Americans as a whole tended to have toward Barack Obama's first presidential campaign versus his second. During the early part of his first campaign, much of the resistance toward voting for him was fear of what was described as "wasting a vote" on someone who the dominant white culture would assure a lost. In other words, history was a warning to Blacks that invested a vote in a non-white candidate; for all practical purposes, such a choice was considered a guaranteed lost and a virtual throwing away of one's ballot.

The campaign appealed mostly to those who were viewed as idealists or naïve, especially non-Black college students who could afford to gamble at great odds due to not being providers for their families or otherwise facing the threat of poverty. It was only after Obama's campaign gained momentum and credibility among certain sectors of the dominant group that significant numbers of African Americans began to believe that he was more than a mere distraction for his Democratic opponent Hillary Clinton.

The economic power and the influence that Oprah Winfrey has over individuals such as middle-class white women that are part of her cult-like television following definitely lent credibility to the Illinois Senator who most of America did not seem to know. Also, his being seen with Oprah drew him closer to her African American viewers. A significant number of Oprah Winfrey's followers of all colors transferred their affections to Obama. Oprah's audience, youthful progressives, and later, Blacks, as well as those who were recently introduced to hardships that are common among people of color, such as massive unemployment among their peers, became enthralled in the Obama campaign's promise of "change."

Some Positive Changes

Obama has brought some positive change to America as a whole. However, as Harry Belafonte states, he has not specifically addressed the plight of African Americans. Belafonte maintains that he will not do so any more willingly than any president of the past has, citing the fact that Dr. King was told by Kennedy that he would have to compel him through the support of the masses to do so. Similarly, Al Sharpton stated in a heated debate against Cornel West that Obama should not be expected to take up the cause of Black liberation like an activist due to his role as the President excluding him from carrying the banner. The president is the antithesis of the Black militant or liberator in that he has sworn to carry on the very system that has been guilty of oppressing African Americans.

Al Sharpton's views are more in line what those of his Democratic peers, whereas Cornel West describes himself as a Democratic Socialist, a member of Democratic Socialists of America. Obama continues to have die-hard supporters among not only staunch Democrats, but those who define themselves as radical, such as Nathan Hare, aka the "Father of Black Studies," who I contacted to ask for a comment to cite in this essay. His response was that Obama is doing a much better job in his role as president than most so-called progressives, black or white, are doing in terms of advancing the cause of radical change in this country. He alluded to the facts that Mitt Romney would have been a nightmare for Blacks, and that Obama was the better candidate, two points with which I agree.

Whereas during the early stages of Obama's first run for office many Blacks were afraid to commit to him due to perceived chances that he would lose, many made a last minute decision to vote for him in 2012 for fear of Romney winning. Many of my peers had vowed not to vote at all as a way of protesting Obama's being "just like any other president" and essentially a disappointment to Blacks. However, a significant number were, in essence, scared to the polls by Mitt Romney's late campaign comments on the forty-seven percent, etc.

Lesser of Two Evils

For the most part, Barack Obama has symbolized the same thing for Blacks as any other candidates that we as a group have supported, i.e. the lesser of two evils. Past presidents, including but not limited to Bill Clinton and Jimmy Carter, have better records of support for the concerns of African Americans as a group. For one, their records relating to imprisonment, which, as stated earlier, is a great concern among Blacks, are unequivocally better than Obama's. According to Christopher Zoukis, the author of Education behind Bars, he entered his second term having granted only twenty-two pardons and one commutation. This contrasts sharply with Jimmy Carter's granting of clemency 566 times and Bill Clinton doing so 459 times. Zoukis points out that: "Even George W. Bush, derided as cruel and uncaring by many on the left, pardoned, commuted, or rescinded the sentences and convictions of 200 men and women during his presidency."

To the question of whether or not Obama's re-election represents advancement in terms of opportunities for black progressives to carry out any sort of black liberation, the answer appears to be that there has been a regression when compared to certain past administrations. Seemingly, Obama is of the opinion that it would not be "politically correct" for him to appear to press the issue of blackness, which suggests that he fears that lame "reverse discrimination" charge that has often been used in reference to Affirmative Action. To further complicate the matter or, in other words, put blinders or rose colored glasses on less informed audiences, Al Sharpton has re-made himself into a prime time media figure that protects Obama from being attacked as would a champion guard dog. He carries the torch and leads the way for Blacks who are for the first time in history preoccupied with the First Family. More so than ever before, Blacks are showing signs of patriotism that resembles that of the dominant culture. Some go as far as to claim that we are living in a post-racial society.

Need for Honest Evaluation

Harry Belafonte is a voice of reason in the midst of the so-called "community," "the African American community," which has been affected by the equivalent of the opiate to which Marx made reference. Faith and hope in Obama as opposed to an honest evaluation of him among African Americans has allowed him to ignore our needs without the protest that would have been directed toward a white President if his or her record were the same. Intoxicated by the image of the seemingly model family that has defied all odds, African Americans, including those who are otherwise progressive, have become content with being short changed, as long as they stand the chance of being a part of such events as the inaugural ball, a glimpse of the First Lady's dress at close proximity, etc. Many have, for all practical purposes, turned in their picket signs for patriotic souvenirs. Such complacency among Blacks is a resident's paradise. Any hope that he will pick up a sign and lead a protest against himself is ridiculous.

As a group, we, i.e,. African American progressives, must stop expecting Barack Obama to lead a revolution against the system of which he is the figurehead. "Change," was the catch-phrase of his first campaign. However, he could not have actually meant it in the true sense of the word, which means "revolution." If so, he would have been accused of attempting to overthrow the system that he swore to uphold as a senator and now as president.

Black progressives have agendas that differ from any one that the Commander- in-Chief of the Armed Forces, aka the president would have, or would even address without being virtually pushed against the wall and forced to acknowledge. In his response to my request for a comment, Nathan Hare, who was known in the sixties as a man of action, having been a key figure in the San Francisco State College uprisings, mentioned that contemporary intellectuals are mostly confining themselves to talk as opposed to taking steps to carry out change. In consideration of his remarks, what are those who are not pleased with Obama's lack of concern for black issues willing to do to carry out change?

What is their action plan as opposed to their mere standpoint? Are we afraid that we will embarrass the first black president if his own people carry out a "March on Washington" with signs that read "Do you care about us?"

Obama has already heard what Harry Belafonte, Cornel West, Louis Far-rakhan, et al have to say about his performance. However, the black masses have been relatively quiet in terms of expressing whatever dismay they have for being essentially overlooked by his administration. The actions that will result in positive change will not be carried out by the president or any leader who at this point is, in essence, no longer part of the masses. Also, unless the intellectuals among us are willing to engage directly with the members of the poor and working-class communities, listening to their points of view as opposed to presenting them with rhetoric that we serve to them from long handled spoons, there will be no change, only what Nathan Hare described in his comments concerning this matter as "intellectual masturbation."

In summation, I will reiterate what I have often said in meetings at the local chapter of the Committees of Correspondence for Democracy and Socialism: Instead of meeting to discuss a meeting about a meeting about a meeting, we need to take devise plans that lend themselves to close to immediate action. Otherwise we are the equivalent of what Huey Newton called "Paper Panthers." To avoid falling into that category, I extend an invitation to all to begin painting signs and preparing for a trip to that white house where that black man lives, now seemingly unaware of our people's plight.

Young People, Emerging Identities and Political Action

By Jimmy Lappe

I fear that, in writing this piece, I am treading upon potentially dangerous ground. Before I begin, I wish to say that I speak only for myself; I do not and cannot purport to speak with any authority on the activism of young people in general. Indeed, to the extent that youth and student organizing can be said to have a center I am certainly positioned somewhere along its periphery, having long ago eschewed traditional campus life for the urban university, and student organizing for the decidedly less youth-oriented spheres of formal politics and the labor movement.

This is perhaps not such a novel approach towards politics, however. Indeed, if we look at the varied forms of activism in which young people are engaged, we will witness, in the first place, that it has no stable center. Furthermore many young people are organizing across identities-that is to say not only, or primarily as students but also or rather as workers, as people of color, as queer/LGBTQ folks, as women, as immigrants, and so on ad infinitum. In general, the activisms of young people potentially offer tremendous opportunities as well as substantial challenges for those of us who hope to build a substantial American Left.

In general, the emerging generation does seem to offer some substantial sources of optimism for the Left. Younger voters were an essential component of Barack Obama's electoral victories in 2008 and 2012, and they played a decisive role in frustrating right-wing objectives and candidates throughout the country during last year's election. Cause for optimism is not limited, however, to the narrow field of electoral politics. A 2010 Pew Research Center report found that younger Americans have a far more positive view of socialism than do older segments of the population. Indeed, for people under 30, socialism and capitalism seem to be held in the same esteem, while for all other age groups capitalism retains a substantial advantage. And, as alluded to above, young people also have a substantial presence in the wide array of struggles and protest movements that have animated left and progressive politics in recent years.

Young people are faced with a truly baffling number of political challenges, and consequently, there is no central premise or issue around which our myriad forms of activism are organized.

As students, we face an educational system that is increasingly in crisis at all levels-from overcrowded elementary schools and school consolidation to a system of higher education that increasingly promises little apart from massive loan debt. Further, many of the programs and institutions designed to make a college education a possibility for lower-income and minority students - programs such as Pell Grants, Federal Student Loans, and affirmative action programs - are and have been under sustained attack from the right for decades.

We're Not All Students, or Only Students

Young people, however, are not all students, and very few are only students. Earlier this year the Census Bureau released a report which found that over 70% of college undergraduates work at least part of the year, and that some 20% of college undergraduates held full-time jobs. Regardless of their status as students, young workers are confronted with a dismal economy, an abysmal job market, declining real wages and limited benefits. Increasingly, young college graduates enter into a labor market that has little need for their skills compelling them to accept work in retail and service industry jobs for which they are formally overqualified.

While school and work are at the center of many young people's lives, the political and social challenges that face young people today are not by any means confined to their roles as students and workers. Young people are also confronted with an increasingly dire ecological crisis, the longest war in U.S. history, the continued exercise of racism and white skin privilege, xenophobia and anti-immigrant hysteria, and the ongoing struggle for GLBT civil rights, to name but a few. These varied struggles serve to shape the political identities of young people and to form similarly varied forms of political activism. Again, we should note that none of these issues, none of these forms of activism, should be understood to have primacy over the others. There is no singular formation or system of activism that uniquely captures a singular youth zeitgeist.

As they have since at least the 1930s, many young people are engaged in activism as students, and for decades the largest national center of student activism has been the United States Student Association. USSA has a very broad mission statement, which includes engaging students in political action, promoting diversity and inclusiveness on university campuses, and making higher education more affordable and accessible to students throughout the United States. In addition to its national lobbying efforts, USSA has a broad network of state student associations throughout the country that organize around state higher education funding and access to education issues. USSA attempts to organize across identities as well and actively builds spaces for minority voices and identity-based activism within the organization. Since 1999, the group has partnered with Jobs with Justice to organize students around workplace justice issues on campuses and in the larger communities where students work and live.

While USSA is the largest and most established center for student organizing in the country, its work only directly touches a small number of students in the country; consequently, there are many other sites of student activism. Outside of USSA, numerous state student associations are involved in college affordability and state funding issues. These associations vary widely in their effectiveness and in their core missions, but many share a basic commitment to building student engagement in political affairs, especially at the state level.

The New SDS

Alongside the work of USSA and state student associations, and inspired by past generations of student activism, a new iteration of Students for a Democratic Society emerged in 2006 to link radical students around the country into a nationwide network. SDS coalesces nationally around access to education issues, but it also seeks to combat varied forms of injustice and oppression. Its decentralized structure allows space for local chapters to engage in varied forms of organizing around issues affecting students both on their campuses and in their broader communities.

Contemporary student organizing, however, is by no means confined to the general organizing undertaken by USSA, SDS, or the state student associations. For over a decade, the United Students against Sweatshops has organized students around worker justice issues - both in the global supply chain, where it seeks to support the organization of garment workers in the Global South, and on college and university campuses, where its affiliates seek to build student support for union organizing and fair contract campaigns. Countless more students are drawn into politics by campus-based identity organizing, which flourishes across the country through various organizations based upon race, ethnicity, sex and sexual identities. Sometimes these groups are tied to national organizations, but just as often they are organized locally on individual campuses. It is far beyond the scope of this article to map out all of the various local campus-based identity struggles, but it is nonetheless important to recognize that they serve as important entry points into the political arena for many young people. Theses struggles also have achieved some important victories, such as broadening university anti-discrimination policies to include GLBT and queer-identified students and winning in-state tuition for undocumented immigrants in a growing number of states.

Despite the broad scope of student-based activism, this work only accounts for but a piece of young people's political activity. Occupy Wall Street and its associated occupations around the country demonstrated that a great many young people are deeply troubled by our nation's dire economic situation and are prepared to take action to change it. If the Occupy movement itself failed to achieve its broad set of demands, its rhetoric of the 99% against the 1% has nonetheless helped to provide a new, at least vaguely class-based frame to organizing in general and to youth organizing in particular.

From Occupy to the Workplace

Spurred at least in part by Occupy, many young people are engaged in a wide array of workplace justice struggles outside of the established labor movement. Low-wage workers - many, but by no means all, of whom are young people -- are engaged in a number of struggles across the country. Some of these struggles are being organized by national networks such as the Restaurant Opportunities Center, the National Guestworker Alliance and OUR Wal-Mart, but at least as often, local networks like New York City's Fast Food Forward and Kansas City's KC 99 are taking the lead in organizing low wage workers. These groups, along with many others around the country, are developing ways to build power for workers who historically have been neglected by organized labor and for whom the protections of the National Labor Relations Act have been elusive at best. There are thousands of other young people who are members of the established labor movement, and while many local and statewide labor councils are beginning to acknowledge the importance of young workers for the future of the labor movement, efforts at young member engagement have been uneven at best.

I have highlighted here some of the organizing work that young people are engaged in as students and as workers because this is the work that I am most familiar with and connected to, but these struggles are by no means the only ones young people are engaged in. Like all people, young people enter into political life in different places and for different reasons, and are very much at the forefront of organizing around a wide

array of other pressing issues.
Young people in general potentially offer a tremendous opportunity for growing and deepening the U.S. Left. But at least in my estimation, the kind of Left that we need must respect and acknowledge that young people - indeed, that all people - have a wide range of political interests and are animated by different issues.

A Left that narrowly sees every struggle as a more-or-less clear vindication of Marx (or, for that matter, of any other favored figure in Left history) cannot adequately address the heterogeneous problems of the 21st century. For all of his importance Marx could not, and did not foresee the rise of the service economy, or the development of identity politics, and consequently there are serious limits to relying too heavily on Marx in contemporary analysis. What we need to build is a Left that respects and encourages difference, that allows for principled disagreements, and that welcomes a wide range of viewpoints, tactics and strategies. A Left that fails to do these things will only manage to grow modestly, and it will attract few supporters among the emerging generations.

Strategic Thinking on the U.S. Six Party System

Congressional Progressive Caucus presenting its platform

"If you know the enemy and know yourself, your victory will not stand in doubt; if you know Heaven and know Earth, you may make your victory complete."

--Sun Tzu, The Art of War

By Carl Davidson
CCDS National Co-Chair

Successful strategic thinking starts with gaining knowledge, particular gaining adequate knowledge of the big picture, of all the political and economic forces involved (Earth) and what they are thinking, about themselves and others, at any given time. (Heaven). It's not a one-shot deal. Since both Heaven and Earth are always changing, strategic thinking must always be kept up to date, reassessed and revised.

To make a political assessment of the forces commanded by the US bourgeoisie and its subaltern allies and strata, it helps to make an examination of Congress, the White House and other Beltway institutions, as well as voting trends and others political and cultural among the masses. And to get an accurate estimation, we must often tear away, set aside or bracket misleading labels and frames, as well as assess varying economic resources and voting results. We want to illuminate an intentionally obfuscated landscape, like when a flash of lightning at night does away with shadows and renders the landscape in sharp relief.

The primary conventional wisdom we want to dissect here is that the US has a two-party system. First, the nature of political parties in the US today is rather unique; they are not parties in any European parliamentary sense, where members are bound to a program or platform with some degree of discipline, and mass party organizations exist at the base. Second, the Republicans and the Democrats in the US are largely empty shells locally, consisting mainly of incumbents and staffers, and their retained lawyers, fundraisers and media consultants. There is some variation from state to state -- state committeemen and women will pass resolutions and certify ballot status and positions, but there's not much of a mass character save for an occasional campaign rally. Third, at the Congressional level the two-party structure, to some degree, still allows for dividing the spoils of committee assignments, but even these are often warped by other considerations.

A few also like to argue that the US has only one party, a capitalist party, with two wings, the bad and the worse. But this is reductionist to a fault, and doesn't tell you much other than that we live in a capitalist society, which is rather trivial.

Some also hold out hope for a "third party" that is noncapitalist. But given the "winner take all" rules in most elections, along with the amount of money and resources required to mount credible campaigns, these are long shots, save for periods of crisis and upheaval, like the period just before the US Civil War, where the Whigs imploded, the Liberty Party had a role, and a new "First Party" formed, the GOP. Another period worth a deeper look is 1944-48, when the rising forces of the Cold War and Southern racism led to a four-way race in 1948 between the Dixiecrats (Strom Thurmond), the Democrats (Harry Truman), the GOP (Thomas Dewey) and the Progressive Party (Henry Wallace).

Our Six-Party System

But today, we'll do better to get a more accurate picture of our adversaries if we set aside the labels of "two-party system", "Democrats" and "Republicans" and the other nuances mentioned above. Instead, I'll offer an alternative working hypothesis, that we live under a six-party system with two labels, and that this will give us a closer and more realistic view of the relation and balance of forces with which we have to deal. But even here, it's important to note that we are discussing "parties" as clusters of colluding and contending blocs of interests, economic views and social coalitions, not unified and disciplined ideological formations strictly bound to a platform. The six "parties" described here below, however, do come closer to these kinds of constructs than the larger "two labels" they operate under.

So who are they?

The Tea Party. So far, only this most far right group has been given the label "party" in the mass media, even though it operates as a faction within the GOP. It generally represents anti-globalist nationalism with a prominence given to the "Austrian School" economics of classical liberalism and, in some cases, the self-interest philosophy of Ayn Rand. It also merges with paleo-conservative traditionalists, which serves as a cover for defending white and male privilege and armed militia groups. It appeals to about 10-20 percent of the electorate, with greater support in the South and West. It is currently locked in a fierce factional struggle with the other wing of the GOP. While a minority in the House overall, they dominate the GOP House Caucus, and thus, as reported widely on 24-hour news cycles, they can and do block many bills from coming to the floor. Tea Party incumbents have been aided in gaining and retaining their seats by GOP-led redistricting on the level of the states they control, breaking up districts electing Democrats and forming new one with more homogenous rightwing majorities. This was begun by Paul Weyrich of the "New Right" under Ronald Reagan, and continues to this day

The Republican Multinationalists. These are the neoliberal money-bags of the GOP (and the neoconservative subset termed "The War Party" by Pat Buchanan and Ron Paul from the right)-the Bushes, Cheney, Karl Rove, the Koch brothers and others with fortunes rooted in petroleum, defense industries and other US businesses with global reach. Their neoliberal economics became hegemonic with Reagan's ascendancy via the anti-Black and anti-feminist "Southern Strategy" alliance with the forces that later came to make up the Tea Party right. The Koch brother's money also helped form ALEC, the American Legislative Exchange Council, thus allowing business lobbyists to write uniform reactionary legislation, mainly on the state level, across the country. Despite statewide gains, the GOP label's current dilemma is that the Tea Party's more inane, backward and proto-fascist views on social and cultural issues is causing the GOP tickets to lose national elections, deadlock the Congress and strain the alliance. On the other hand, if the "Country Club" Republicans dump the Tea Party, the GOP itself may implode

The Blue Dogs. This caucus in the Democratic Party is tied to "Red State" mass voting bases - the military industrial workers, and the Southern and Appalachian regions. They are neo-Keynesian on military matters, but neoliberal on everything else. Their "party" frequently sides with the GOP in Congressional voting. The Blue Dog Coalition has recently shrunk from 27 to 14 members, often having paved the way to self-defeat by backhandedly encouraging GOP victories in their districts by attacking Obama and other Democrats.

The "Third Way" New Democrats. This "party" of the center right is mainly the US electoral arm of global and finance capital, with the Clintons and Rahm Emanuel as the better known public faces. Formed to break with "economic populism" of the old FDR coalition, and assert a variety of globalist "free trade" measures and the gutting of Glass-Steagall banking regulations, this new post-Reagan-Mondale grouping decided to put distance between itself and traditional labor allies. While neo-Keynesian on most matters, it also "triangulates" with neoliberal positions. This was started as the Democratic Leader Council and the "New Democrat" Coaltions. John Kerry is a member of the DLC, but President Obama has claimed "no direct connection," even though the grouping lists him as one of its "rising stars." The DLC/ "New Democrats" essentially speaks for some of the more powerful elements of finance capital under the "Democratic" label. It is the dominant view among the Senate Democratic majority.

Old New Dealers.   This "party" is represented by unofficial wealthy Democratic groups like Americans Coming Together, plus the AFL-CIO's Committee on Political Education and others. They take a Keynesian approach to economic matters, and are often critical of finance capital and the trade deals promoted by the globalists. They are also wary of deep defense cuts that would cause layoffs among their membership base. They maintain, however, strong alliances with some civil rights, women's and environmental groups. Their main value to Democratic tickets is their independent get-out-the-vote operations, which can be decisive in many races. They also work closely with the Alliance for American Manufacturing, a business-based anti-free trade lobby that works with labor.

PDA/Congressional Progressive Caucus. While the largest single caucus in the House, the CPC "party" is still relatively small, representing 80 out of 435 votes. Its policy views are Keynesian and, in some cases, social-democratic as well. Its recent "Back-to-Work Budget" serves as an excellent economic platform for a popular front against finance capital. It also largely overlaps with the Hispanic and Black Caucuses, and is the most multinational "Rainbow" grouping in the Congress. It also includes Senator Bernie Sanders, the sole socialist in Congress, who was an initial founder of the CPC. It has opposed the wars in Iraq and Afghanistan, under the Progressive Democrats of America banners of "Healthcare Not Warfare" and "Windmills Not Weapons." It has recently gained some direct union support from the militant National Nurses United and the Communications Workers of America. Many, but not all, CPC members are also members of Progressive Democrats of America, an independent PAC dubbed the "Tom Hayden/ Dennis Kucinich" Democrats at the time of their founding in 2004. The Congressional Progressive Caucus is the closest political group the US has that would parallel some of the "United Left" socialist and social democratic groups in European countries.

What Does It All Mean?

With this brief descriptive and analytical mapping of the upper crust of American politics, many things begin to fall in place. Romney, a very wealthy representative of the Multinational GOP group, defeated all the Tea Party candidates in the primaries, and consequently, could never convince the Tea Party he was one of them, simply because he wasn't. This led to a drop in GOP voter enthusiasm that couldn't even be overcome with 'dog whistle' appeals to racism and revanchism in the campaigns.

The Obama administration, on the other hand, at its core, represents an alliance between the DLC "Third Way" and the "Old New Dealers," while also pulling along the PDA/Congressional Progressive Caucus as energetic but critical secondary allies. The Blue Dogs found themselves out in the cold from the wider Obama coalition, and shrank accordingly. Barbara Lee of PDA and the CPC, moving from a minority of one on Afghanistan at the start of the invasion, finally got a majority of House Democrats to oppose and push Obama on the wars, but to little avail in any immediate sense, being thwarted by both the DLC and the Multinational GOP.

This "big picture" also reveals much about the current budget debates, which are shown to be three-sided-the extreme austerity neoliberalism of the Tea Party Ryan budget, the "austerity lite" budget of the DLC-dominated Senate Democrats, and the left Keynesian progressive "Back-to-Work" budget of the Congressional Progressive Caucus. The "Old New Dealers" were caught in the middle, with only 20 or so coming over on the Black Caucus version of the "Back-to-Work" budget, which was still in the minority.

While all this shows why and how Obama was able to pull together a majority electoral coalition, it also reveals why he is still thwarted on pulling together an effective governing coalition. Likewise, it shows how the Tea Party, with only 10-20 percent of the electorate, is able to water down or completely bloc common-sense measures on gun control with 70-90 percent support among the general population.

Finally, the fact that there is only one avowed socialist in Congress tells us something about our own position in the overall balance of forces. Socialist candidates are only able to draw 2% to 5% of the votes in this period, save for Sanders, and we all know that Vermont has some unique features that made it possible, not that Sanders didn't do yeoman work in pulling together a progressive majority that elected him.

In summary, here are a few things to keep in mind. If you decide to intervene in electoral work to build independent working class grassroots organizations, you don't go "inside the Democratic Party". There's not much of an "inside" there anymore. What you do instead is join or work with one of the two factions/ "parties" that are left of center. Your aim is to make either of these stronger, preferably the PDA/Congressional Progressive Caucus. Then to shift the overall balance of forces, your task is to defeat the Tea Party, the Multinational GOP, and the Blue Dogs. At present, not a single piece of progressive legislation is going to get passed without driving a wedge between the two parties under the GOP label and weakening both of them.

We have to keep in mind however, that "shifting the balance of forces" is mainly an indirect and somewhat ephemeral gain. It does "open up space", but for what? Progressive initiatives matter for sure, but much more is required strategically. We are interested in pushing the popular front vs. finance capital to its limits, and within that effort, developing a socialist bloc. If that comes to scale, the "Democratic Party Tent" is likely to collapse and implode, given the sharper class contractions and other fault lines that lie within it, much as the Whigs did in the 19th Century. That demands an ability to regroup all the progressive forces into a new "First Party" alliance able to contend for power.

An old classic formula summing up the strategic thinking of the united front and popular front is appropriate here: "Unite and develop the progressive forces, win over the middle forces, isolate and divide the backward forces, then crush our adversaries one by one." In short, we have to have a policy and set of tactics for each one of these elements, as well as a strategy for dealing with them overall. Finally, a note of warning from the futurist Alvin Toffler: "If you don't have a strategy, you're part of someone else's strategy."

The Empire in Disarray: Global Challenges to the International Order

By Harry Targ

A whole generation of activists have politically "grown up" conversant with the central place of empire in human history. Children of the Cold War and the "sixties" generation realized that the United States was the latest of a multiplicity of imperial powers who sought to dominate and control human beings, physical space, natural resources, and human labor power. We learned from the Marxist tradition, radical historians, scholar/activists with historical roots in Africa, and revolutionaries from the Philippines and Vietnam to Southern Africa, to Latin America. We tended to accept the view that imperialism was hegemonic.

A "theory of imperialism" for the 21st century should include four interconnected variables that explain empire building and responses to it. First, as an original motivation for empire, economic interests are primary. The most recent imperial power, the United States, needed to secure customers for its products, outlets for manufacturing investment opportunities, an open door for financial speculation, and vital natural resources such as oil.

Second, geopolitics and military control parallel and support the pursuit of economic domination. The United States, beginning in the 1890s, built a two-ocean navy to become a Pacific power as well as a Western Hemisphere power. The "Asian pivot" of the 21st century and continued opposition to the Cuban and Bolivarian revolutions reflect the one hundred year extension of the convergence of economics and geopolitics in US foreign policy.

Third, as imperial nations flex their muscles on the world stage they need to rationalize exploitation and military brutality to convince others and their own citizens of the humanistic goals they wish to achieve. In short, ideology matters. In the US case "manifest destiny" and the "city on the hill" have been embedded in the dominant national narrative of the country for 150 years.

However, what has often been missing from the leftwing theoretical calculus is an understanding of resistance. Latin American and African dependency theorists and "bottom-up" historians have argued for a long time that resistance must be part of the understanding of any theory of imperialism. In fact, the imperial system is directly related to the level of resistance the imperial power encounters.

Resistance generates more attempts at economic hegemony, political subversion, the application of military power, and patterns of "humanitarian interventionism" and diplomatic techniques called "soft power" today to defuse resistance. But as recent events suggest, resistance of various kinds is spreading throughout global society.

People's History

The impetus for adding resistance to any understanding of imperialism has many sources including Howard Zinn's seminal history of popular movements in the United States, The Peoples History of the United States. Zinn argued convincingly that in each period of American history, ruling class rule was challenged, shaped, weakened, and in a few cases defeated because of movements of indigenous people, workers, women, people of color, middle class progressives and others who stood up to challenge the status quo.

More recently, Vijay Prashad, The Darker Nations, compiled a narrative of post-World War II international relations that highlighted the resistance from the Global South. World history was as much shaped by anti-colonial movements, the construction of the non-aligned movement, conferences and programs supporting liberation struggles and women's rights, as it was by big power contestation. The Prashad book was subtitled "A Peoples History of the Third World."

The 21st century has witnessed a variety of forms of resistance to global hegemony and the perpetuation of neo-liberal globalization all across the face of the globe. First, various forms of systemic resistance have emerged. These often emphasize the reconfiguration of nation-states and their relationships that have long been ignored. The two largest economies in the world, China and India, have experienced economic growth rates well in excess of the industrial capitalist countries. China has developed a global export and investment program in Latin America and Africa that exceeds that of the United States and Europe.

In addition, the rising economic powers have begun a process of global institution building to rework the international economic institutions and rules of decision-making on the world stage. On March 26-27, 2013 the BRICS met in Durban, South Africa. While critical of BRICS shortcomings, Patrick Bond, Senior Professor of Development Studies and director of the University of KwaZulu-Natal Centre for Civil Society, in a collection of readings on the subject introduces BRICS:

In Durban, five heads of state meet to assure the rest of Africa that their countries' corporations are better investors in infrastructure, mining, oil and agriculture than the traditional European and US multinationals. The Brazil-Russia-India-China-South Africa summit also includes 16 heads of state from Africa, including notorious tyrants. A new 'BRICS bank' will probably be launched. There will be more talk about monetary alternatives to the US dollar."

On the South American continent, most residents of the region are mourning the death of Hugo Chavez, the leader of the Bolivarian Revolution. Under Chavez's leadership, inspiration, and support from oil revenues, Venezuela launched the latest round of state resistance to the colossus of the north, the United States. Along with the world's third largest trade bloc MERCOSUR (Argentina, Brazil, Paraguay, Uruguay, and associate memberships including Venezuela and Chile), Latin Americans have participated in the construction of financial institutions and economic assistance programs to challenge the traditional hegemony of the International Monetary Fund, the World Bank, and the World Trade Organization.

Bolivarian Revolution

The Bolivarian Revolution also has stimulated spreading political change based on various degrees of grassroots democratization, the construction of workers' cooperatives, and a shift from neoliberal economic policy to economic populism. With a growing web of participants, Bolivia, Ecuador, Brazil, Argentina, Uruguay, Nicaragua, El Salvador, and, of course, Cuba, the tragic loss of Chavez will not mean the end to the Bolivarian Revolution. It might lead to its deepening.

But the story of 21st century resistance is not just about countries, alliances, new economic institutions that mimic the old. Grassroots social movements have been spreading like wild fire all across the face of the globe. The story can begin in many places and at various times: the new social movements of the 1980s, the Zapatistas of the 1990s, the anti-globalization/anti-IMF campaigns going back to the 1960s and continuing off and on until the new century, and repeated mass mobilizations against a Free Trade Agreement for the Americas.

Since 2011, the world has been inspired by Arab Spring, workers mobilizations all across the industrial heartland of the United States, student strikes in Quebec, the state of California and in Santiago, Chile. Beginning in 2001 mass organizations from around the world began to assemble in Porto Allegre, Brazil billing their meeting of some 10,000 strong, the World Social Forum. They did not wish to create a common political program. They wished to launch a global social movement where ideas are shared, issues and demands from the base of societies could be raised, and in general the neoliberal global agenda reinforced at the World Economic Forum in Switzerland could be challenged.

Since 2001, the World Social Forum has assembled in Latin America, Asia, Africa, and the United States. Most recently, the last week in March, 2013, 50,000 people from 5,000 organizations in 127 countries from five continents meet in Tunis, the site of the protest that sparked Arab Spring in 2011. Planners wanted to bring mass movements from the Middle East and North Africa into the collective narrative of this global mobilization. As Medea Benjamin reports, this Social Forum was the first to have a "dedicated 'Climate space' to emphasize 'food sovereignty, water justice and respect for the rights of indigenous and forest peoples. Session rejected 'false solutions" put forward by governments that would not solve the environmental crises facing humankind.

Benjamin reported that a Tunisian student, when asked whether the Social Forum movement should continue, answered in the affirmative. The student paid homage to the Tunisian street vendor, Mohamed Bouazizi, who committed suicide and launched Arab Spring and declared that "for all those who have died struggling for justice, we must continue to learn from each other how to build a world that does not respond to the greed of dictators, bankers or corporations, but to the needs of simple people like Mohamed Bouazizi."

Economic Development Strategies of 20th Century Socialism and Lessons for the 21st century

By Duncan McFarland

Introduction: T The Socialist Vision of Marx and Engels

Marx's masterwork Capital was a critique of capitalist production. Earlier, in the Communist Manifesto, Marx and Engels put forward a new theory of history as advancing levels of higher organization based on the mode of production and driven by class struggle. Historical and dialectical materialism was developed from a critique of German and Western philosophy and provided a new method and theory of knowledge.

While there had been socialist theories since the French Revolution, the scientific socialism of Marx and Engels foresaw a new society led by the working class that provided benefits to the large majority, based on the principle "From each according to their ability, to each according to their work." As socialist society advanced with more sophisticated culture and technology, the state would wither away and eventually socialism would transition to the classless, advanced communist society of the future.

The advent of communism will also mark the transition from the epoch of class society -- which started perhaps 6000 years ago with the emergence of agricultural surplus, cities and ancient slave societies -- to the epoch of advanced classless society. This transition will be far deeper and more profound than even the transition from capitalism to socialism.

Experience of the revolutions of the 19th century led Marx and Engels to advance the concept "dictatorship of the proletariat." That is, the state in the socialist period would be the expression of the interests of the working class in the role of a ruling class necessarily advancing its inter-

ests and those of allied classes and suppressing attempts at capitalist restoration. This phrase did not refer to a personal dictatorship.
Political organizations would be needed to fight for power, thus Marx led the formation of the First International in the 1860s and Engels later put much work into the German Social Democratic Party. Marx and Engels also supported the organizing efforts of the contemporary labor movement despite opposition from some quarters that unions were reformist in their purpose and goals.

Thus Marx and Engels produced a new theory of history, philosophy and political economy that was unprecedented in its huge scope, explanatory power and practical method; and they contributed greatly to the formation of entirely new types of revolutionary organizations. The fundamental theoretical problems facing the working class and people during the historical period of capitalism were defined and basically solved by Marx. Since then, the task has been implementation in particular circumstances and therefore development of the theory according to new historical conditions, such as the rise of imperialism, finance capital and problems of socialist construction

With all that accomplishment, however, Marx provided little detail as to what a socialist society would look like. A rigorous materialist, he was not prepared to describe a situation which existed only in the future. General considerations for what Marx and Engels were thinking about, however, are indicated in some places such as the Program for the German Communist Party published in 1848 at the beginning of the year of revolution. (Note this is a short program for the Germans, not the much longer, more universal Communist Manifesto).   The Program for the German Communists proposes an economic program with state ownership of the banks and major industries, as well as collective farms. Obviously there was no opportunity in the lifetime of Marx and Engels to actually implement this program and there is no practical detail at all as to how these proposals would actually work.

The Paris Commune

Marx anticipated that the first proletarian revolutions would happen in the countries with the most developed industrial production and numerous working class,, namely, Britain, France and Germany. This seemed to be the trend with the victory of the Paris Commune and the subsequent organization of a powerful German Social Democratic Party later in the century based on Germany's rapidly expanding industry.

The short-lived Paris Commune did not have the opportunity to unfold an economic development program and did not nationalize the Bank of

France. The German Social Democratic Party, after the death of Engels, became right opportunist in its politics and mostly joined with German imperialism at the advent of World War I, a gigantic betrayal of the working class.

The Russian Revolution

Plekanhov translated Marx's works into Russian, and revolutionary and Marxist activity increased in late 19th century Russia, as the antiquated, backward and reactionary character of the semi-feudal Tsardom was quite apparent. Lenin and his Marxist comrades, while enthusiastically embracing the Marxist theory, found themselves in a situation quite different than had been supposed by Marx. While modern capitalist industry had rapidly developed in a small number of urban areas such as St. Petersburg and Moscow, most of the Russian empire was rural, technologically backward and illiterate. The Tsar was an absolute monarch and there was no constitution, civil liberties or parliament such as existed in the West European countries.

In Germany the Social Democratic Party functioned legally and openopenlyly., in In Russia, however, such activity was strictly prohibited and revolutionaries were subject to arrest, exile or execution. Lenin, therefore, called for a "proletarian party of a new type" -- that is, something different from the at-the-time highly successful German Social Democrats, the leading Marxist party in the world. Lenin structured the Bolshevik Party on the basis of democratic centralism and devised a tightly organized, militant party able to operate underground to avoid Tsarist repression.

The October Revolution in Russia: Stages of Economic Policy

That Lenin's organizational methods were appropriate for Russia was proved by the Bolshevik victory and seizure of power in October of 1917. Having achieved this great political success, however, the Bolsheviks were immediately confronted with the gigantic task of actually governing the country. Foremost of those tasks wasere withdrawing Russia from the disastrous world war and reorganizing and administering the economy.

The Bolsheviks in the fight for power had paid little attention to economic issues.; Ffurthermore, they found themselves in charge not of an advanced industrial economy, as had been suggested by the Marxist theory, but rather a mixed and largely backward economy, with a huge rural, semi-feudal sector.

  a) In the period right after the seizure of power, the Bolsheviks adopted a cautious approach in their economic measures and decrees.

Nationalization was confined to strategic sectors such as finance, internal transportation infrastructure and foreign trade.

Rather than wholesale reorganization of the economy along socialist principles, the Bolsheviks adopted a cautious approach to reorganizing the economy with emphasis on the practical necessity of keeping economic activity going rather than disrupting production with major, innovative changes.

b) Wwith the advent of the civil war in 1918, Bolshevik economic policy changed to "war communism." Decision- making was highly centralized, as a command economy was required for the urgent needs of the military in fighting a civil war and repulsing the foreign capitalist/ imperialist invasion. Grain was requisitioned from the peasants.

c) Wwith the victory in the civil war and the transition to the post-war period, however, the command economy proved inappropriate and unacceptable for normal, peacetime life. The Russian peasants resisted and agricultural production plummeted. Famine emerged and the sailors revolted at Kronstadt. There was rising opposition to Bolshevik rule among the Russian people.

Enter the NEP

At the 10th Party Congress in 1921, Lenin led the Bolsheviks in adopting a new set of economic measures that become known as the New Economic Policy. Incentives were restored in the rural economy through the Tax in Kind. The NEP was a mixed economy; while the Bolsheviks controlled the "commanding heights" - -- finance, heavy industry, transportation, foreign trade --- while a capitalistic free market was restored in the countryside for agriculture, trade and light industry. Addressing the better off peasants, Bukharin said "go enrich yourselves," a phrase that may have been politically not astute but economically accurate. Indeed, the NEP led to an economic recovery in the Soviet Union in the 1920s and restored the people's confidence in the new Communist government.

The NEP was necessary because in an unevenly developed, largely backward and semi-feudal Russia, the historically progressive economic developments of the capitalist system had mostly not been realized. Capitalism brought great progress in relationship to feudalism: a national market, population shift from rural to urban, rational business procedures, modern science and technology, a basically educated work force, production using the division of labor and the new system of factories and industry. Emerging from feudalism, capitalism created international markets and expanded trade, vastly increased the productive forces and generated the new working class. Capitalism also brought forth new forms of exploitation and eventually lost its progressive character and began to degeneratdegenerate.e, theAt that time of the birth of socialist forces began to emerge.

In Marxist theory, capitalist development is the basis to the transition to socialism. Most capitalist development had not occurred, or partially occurred in Tsarist Russia.; Tthe new Communist Party could not create an advanced socialist economy out of ideology and willpower., Tthe necessary economic preconditions were not in place, and it was the job of NEP to put them in place. Capitalist economic development especially in rural areas was both promoted and regulated by the socialist state in Moscow.

The NEP was envisioned originally as a "temporary retreat" but close reading of Lenin's last works, written during the early 1920s, show that he progressively realized that the mixed economy of NEP would need to be in place for a long period of time; at one point, Lenin concluded "for several generations, but not hundreds of years."

While Bukharin, Rykov (premier) and Tomsky (head of trade unions) championed the NEP during the 1920s, many Ccommunist Pparty leaders were uncomfortable with the mixed economy policy. They had not engaged in a generation of bitter struggle only to promote capitalism in the countryside. They witnessed the rising strength of the kulaks, the rich peasants, who exploited the poor peasantry. How could communism be compatible with promoting a system of exploitation? When the communists examined the classic works of Marx and Engels for what little guidance they could find, they found reference not only to state ownership of industry but to state-run collective farming and support for the notion of a "peasant war" in alliance with the workers. Therefore, they thought, NEP was a temporary economic retreat made necessary by the extreme conditions prevailing after the end of the civil war; it was not a long-term policy.

Stalin knew that the majority position among the Communist leaders by the late 1920's was to call off NEP and resume the rapid advance to socialist construction. Thus Stalin attacked and defeated the "Right Opposition" led by Bukharin, and eliminated the NEP group from top party positions. Stalin embarked on the crash program of the first Five Year Plan, with extremely rapid development of heavy industry and collectivization of agriculture in the countryside.

While an increase in the tempo of industrial development may have been good policy, especially because of the hostility and encirclement of the capitalist powers, the more balanced one- and two- year plans advocated by the right opposition made more sense. Very clear, however, was the huge mistake of the forced collectivization of the Russian peasantry. This led to a breach of the worker/peasant alliance and weakening of the political position of the Communist Party among the Russian people.

The "left" errors in the economic policy of the first Five Year Plan were perhaps understandable given that the Bolshevik leadership was blazing a historically unprecedented path and that the policies seemed in accord with Marxist theory. That they were persisted in despite huge problems was due to the destruction of democracy by the Stalin dictatorship and consequent inability of the communist leadership to effectively criticize Stalin's mistake's and make necessary adjustments, including limiting Stalin's power. The five-year plans of the 1930s had tremendous accomplishments in expanding Soviet industry and technology amidst the Great Depression of the capitalist world, but this approach proved unsustainable in the long run. Stalin's policies led to a disruption of the worker/peasant alliance and an unbalanced, over-centralized, top-down, rigid bureaucratic system which was unresponsive to the people and eventually collapsed in the Gorbachev period.

Economic Policies of the Chinese Communist Party of China

Chinese Ccommunists organized the Chinese Communist Party of China in Shanghai in 1921, stimulated by the tremendous impact of the Bolshevik victory in Russia. China's population was a huge and mostly rural population. CPC strategies in the 1920s were closely linked to the Comintern and largely failed.; Mao Zedong changed the strategy to a focus on organizing the peasantry and led the Long March in 1935. The CPC eventually controlled and administered a large liberated zone in northwest China centered on Yanan.

The political and economic policy of the Communists at Yanan was called New Democracy. It was based on a very broad alliance that incorporated not only workers, peasants, and middle class progressives, but also patriotic capitalists. The national or patriotic big bourgeoisie were an important part of New Democracy especially with the advent of the all-out Japanese invasion of China in July 1937. The only sector excluded from the New Democracy alliance was the comprador bourgeoisie or those Chinese who collaborated or sided with the Japanese invaders. In the countryside the communists practiced rent reduction, land reform and redistribution to the peasantry.

With the victory of the Communist forces and subsequent period of economic rehabilitation after decades of war, the Chinese Ccommunists in the 1950s organized a step-by-step creation of socialist economy largely based on the Soviet model. The Party nationalized heavy industry and methodically introduced collective relations in the rural economy. A second phase began along with the breach with the Soviet Union: the Great Leap Forward of 1958 introduced rural communes based on advanced Ccommunist principles. After the failure of the Leap and retrenchment of the early1960s, the Great Proletarian Cultural Revolution in 1966 surged ahead to again champion Ccommunism and the commune system. In Mao's last years, while the principles of the Cultural Revolution were still upheld, the situation stabilized.

Deng Xiaoping came to power in 1978 with a Chinese economy having built a basic, all-round industrial base that was nonetheless technically out-dated with a stagnant rural economy. Ownership was almost exclusively in state and collective hands and the market was greatly limited. In December. 1978, China adopted an economic reform policy which began with de-collectivizing the rural economy, as China's peasants embraced the system of family contract farming with great enthusiasm and mostly left the communes. Success of the early reforms led to their extension and growth of the free market. The program to construct Special Economic Zones and introduce large scale foreign investment from Japan, the US, Europe and overseas Chinese was also a major success. Within a few years the Chinese had constructed an economy that bore resemblance to the Soviet NEP economy of the 1920s: state ownership of finance, heavy industry and strategic national industries with a burgeoning capitalistic sector of private businesses and (particular to China) export-oriented industries. China's economic program of reform and opening up did have the advantage over Soviet NEP in that a generation of economic development had created a solid industrial basis.

By the ascension of power of Hu Jintao at the 16th Party Congress of 2002, the limitations of Chinese economic reforms were becoming quite apparent to both the Chinese people and the Communist leadership. Having built powerful production forces, it was time to shift to a more balanced economic model and deal deal with problems such as the income gap, exploitation of labor, hardships of migrant workers and pollution.

Vietnam

After the victory over US imperialism and their South Vietnamese partners, a reunited Vietnam in 1975 decided on an economic development program based on the Soviet model. While providing social services on an egalitarian basis, this system did not work to develop the productive forces -- Vietnam in ten years changed from a rice-exporting to a rice importing country, there was hunger and people were very dissatisfied. The problem was that the advanced socialist relations of production were too far ahead of the still largely backward economic basis.

Vietnam adopted the Doi Moi policy of economic renewal in 1986.; Doi Moi created a mixed economy with the state controlling strategic economic sectors with the free market restored for smaller scale private enterprise and a major program of foreign investment for export production. The Vietnamese economy rapidly improved and the country became the second largest rice exporter in the world. However,There there are serious problems such as corruption and , bureaucracy and inflation.

Cuba

Cuba adopted a Soviet style economy in the 1970s and 1980s but major dissatisfactions led to a rectification program being adopted in 1986. The efforts to reform the economy were cut short by the shock and depression resulting from the collapse of socialism in the Soviet Union and the Eastern European countries, leading to the "special period" in Cuba of the 1990s. By around 2005 Cuba had restored normalcy -- basic needs such as food and medical care were taken care of for the Cuban people. However, the task of building a modern, prosperous and technically advanced economy still remained. After a huge national program of consultation, a set of guidelines were adopted to move things forward; Cuba sought to energize and expand private employment, cooperatives of different types and private farming to complement the dominant state sector. With the state ownership still dominant, more diverse economic sectors are being developed.

Some Conclusions

Communist Parties in the 20th century won state power and became ruling parties in the "weak link," least developed of the European powers, namely Russia; and in developing countries of the Third World, namely China, Vietnam and Cuba. There was no instance of a Ccommunist -Pparty- led socialist revolution winning victory in an advanced industrial country such as originally envisioned by Marx and Engels. Consequently, ruling parties were required to develop economic development programs in conditions which includeding major semi-feudal or pre-capitalist elements, where the historically beneficial and necessary features of capitalist development in relation to feudalism had not yet occurred.

The Soviet NEP was the first to respond to these conditions by the creation of a mixed development strategy with the Communist Party in a controlling position holding political power in a one-party state, dominant in economic policy with a state run strategic sector (e.g. finance and heavy industry) while expanding capitalistic development in agriculture, light industry, trade and some industry.

China, Vietnam and now Cuba have all referenced this model while adapting it to their national conditions. This approach had the contradictory feature of developing socialism and capitalism at the same time, with socialism in control. Learning from the fall of the Soviet Union, the possibility of the overthrow of the socialist power is a real danger if mistakes are not corrected.

The Global Balance of Forces

US Imperialism remains the center of world capitalism and seeks to maintain a strategic position of dominance. US imperialism, however, is in a state of decline, losing economic vitality and political influence. Consequently, the US more and more relies on its military power to pursue its ambitious strategic agenda.

However, much of the world today is resisting US dominance or simply developing in a different direction. Since "9/11", left and progressive forces in Latin America have asserted themselves and US control of its "backyard" has been broken. The BRICS countries (Brazil, Russia, India, China and South Africa) have emerged as a significant influence and the "Arab Spring" in North Africa has seen rising forces of democracy and youth and contributed to the slipping position of Israel. The US imperial project in Iraq failed albeit with colossal damage to the country and its people, and the war in Afghanistan haswas also been a failure.

If China, Vietnam and Cuba are led by Ccommunist pparties more-or-less correctly developing socialist economies according to the specific conditions of their countries, then the global forces of socialism are far more powerful than often assessed by the gloomy picture presented by the US left. China's rise, because of its huge size and economic success, has become a major obstacle to US imperialism. The US is particularly alarmed as most economists predict that China's economy will surpass the US by mid-century to become the world's largest. This is an important factor in the strategic "pivot" of US imperialism to the Asia/Pacific region, a strategy articulated in a Jan.nuary 2012 paper signed by Defense Secretary Panetta and President Obama and since implemented by numerous moves. Thus US imperialism begins the 21st century with a strategy of encircling and containing China. The Chinese response is to create global economic ties in Africa, Latin America, and the rest of the

world, as well as to maintain a strong policy of defending its sovereignty
and border regions.

Thus, in summary, world capitalist/imperialist forces led by the US maintain an aggressive external military posture seeking hegemony but are
declining in strength. World progressive, left and socialist forces are
increasing in power. How this contradiction unfolds -- whether it leads
to a major confrontation or war --- is a major historic issue for the 21st
century.

Lessons and Looking Forward

Communist parties took state power in a number of countries in the
20th century and implemented economic development programs. The
Soviet Union and China achieved rapid industrialization and modernization with success comparable if not better than the best performances of
capitalist industrialization, e.g., Great Britain, the US, Germany, Japan.

This vast experience provides persuasive confirmation in practice of
the theory of Marxist political economy, which in addition continues
to provide the best explanation of surplus value and capitalist production. Consequently, 21st century socialism must continue to be based
on Marxism or scientific socialism, while at the same time growing to
include new and emerging historical trends.

The economic problems, setbacks and failures of 20th century socialism
were also vast, and a rapid advance from capitalism to advanced socialism or communism proved impossible. The dialectical relationship
between economic development and good political leadership assumed
great importance.

The Soviet model, starting with the 5-year plans proved unsustainable;
over-centralized, inefficient and bureaucraticc. iit suffered from poor
performance in agriculture and consumer goods. The top-down, undemocratic political process made correcting errors very difficult.

Planning based on the assumption of advanced socialist relations did not
match the more backward reality. China, Vietnam and Cuba all adopted
the Soviet model but made major changes when the model proved inadequate or unworkable. With large semi-feudal areas, these countries
were more backward than the situation envisioned by Marx. China and
Vietnam developed more a appropriate socialist market economy, with
capitalistic and socialist features, but led by a communist party guiding
the development towards socialism.

Cuba is still experimenting to find the way forward. All three countries
emphasize that there is no formula for economic development; Marxist

principles must be applied to the specific historical conditions of their countries. China in particular with its huge size and deep history has built a powerful and dynamic economy. At no time should success permit the hubris that may lead to capitalist restoration.

US Marxists need to pay attention to the lessons of history and have a more open attitude towards the communist-led, socialist market economies. The US Marxists, when painting athe picture or telling a story about 21st century socialism in their countrythe US, will need to portray a society that is more democratic, participatory, humane and creative. Furthercreative than the Soviet Union. However, living in a developed bourgeois industrial society, the US Marxists will likely project more advanced social relations than in the socialist market economies. Barring global catastrophe such as nuclear war or earth climate disaster, Marxism still predicts the eventual triumph of socialism in the US and throughout the world.

Duncan McFarland is a CCDS National Committee member and chairs its Peace and Solidarity Committee.

Creating an Ecological Civilization

By Jiang Chunyun

From: English Edition of Qiushi Journal. A publication of the Chinese Communist Party Central Committee, Vol.5, No.1, January 1, 2013

As the old Chinese proverb goes, "To return a kindness with gratitude is a good deed, the act of an upright man; to treat a kindness with ingratitude is a bad deed, the act of a petty man." These words, "good" and "bad," "gratitude" and "ingratitude," have long been the most fundamental criteria for judging the morality and action of an individual. Do children treat their parents with respect out of gratitude for the loving care their parents have given them? Do countrymen serve their motherland wholeheartedly out of gratitude for everything their motherland has afforded them? And do human beings have awe for and cherish their green home out of gratitude for the life that nature has granted them? Everybody on earth, individuals and groups alike, must find rational answers to these questions, regardless of their nationality, race, gender, class, and occupation, and must require both themselves and others to act in accordance with a just code of speaking out for good and doing good instead of evil.

Life on earth began as early as several hundred million years ago, while the story of human evolution started only several million years ago. This means that humans are latecomers. At every step of human evolution— from our transformation from Australopithecus to Homo erectus, and again from archaic Homo sapiens to Homo sapiens—we have been cared for by nature, which, like a great and holy mother, has allowed humankind to grow from a species with few members to one with several billion members. In comparison with family and country, the care that nature has bestowed on us is more fundamental, more worthy of our gratitude. Yet how have we treated nature? This may be a difficult question to answer, but it is one that we must answer as a matter of conscience.

Frankly speaking, there are many people who are able to show appreciation towards nature. These people have made active contributions to ecological protection and the improvement of the environment. But at the same time, there are also people who have no sense of gratitude towards nature. These people are indifferent towards the changes that are affecting nature and the environment. Moreover, there are even people who are so ungrateful towards nature that they would wantonly damage the environment. These people are by no means few in number, and their violations against nature are on the increase. This is the root cause of the ecological degradation and environmental deterioration that has plunged the human race into a survival crisis.

Industrial Revolution Brings Significant Damage

Ecological and environmental issues began to emerge with the advent of agricultural society, although at that time the impact of human activities on the environment was gradual and relatively minor. However, with the arrival of the Industrial Revolution and the rapid development of science and technology, human beings began to deal serious damage to the environment as they created great material wealth and cultural achievements. This damage has become increasingly serious in modern times. Air pollution, water pollution, soil pollution, desertification, global warming, the melting of the glaciers, the depletion of the ozone, the spread of acid rain, the sharp drop in biodiversity, and the frequent occurrence of fatal diseases and natural disasters—these startling facts are a warning that the earth's biosphere, which mankind relies on for its survival, is damaged. They tell us that the major ecological systems supporting the earth's biosphere, such as forests, grasslands, wetlands, rivers, lakes, farmlands, mountains, the atmosphere, and oceans, are bruised all over, weakened, and that untold dangers lurk amongst them. The biosphere is like a cracked fish tank which is losing its water. As the water seeps out of the tank at an increasing rate, the survival of the fish inside is coming under threat. Therefore, if we are unable to repair the biosphere quickly, the damage will only become worse and worse. This will continue until the biosphere eventually ceases to function, being no longer able to operate, and when that happens humankind will descend into a desperate struggle for its survival. This is not alarmist talk, but a real depiction of a hidden crisis that will threaten the survival of the human race.

In an effort to address the human crisis that has been triggered by environmental deterioration, the international community and the countries of the world have frequently convened meetings, signed conventions and accords, issued declarations, made commitments, and taken action. While in some cases these efforts have led to positive results, in overall terms our efforts to restore ecosystems and rectify environments have yielded few results. At most we can say that there has been partial improvement. The trend of environmental deterioration on a global scale is yet to be reversed, and there are even signs that it is becoming more serious. James Speth, the Dean of the School of Forestry and Environmental Studies at Yale University and former Administrator of the United Nations Development Program, says that the trend of environmental decline, which has made the international community uneasy, is yet to be fundamentally mitigated. Ill omens still exist, and these problems are becoming more ingrained, bringing about immediate danger. Speth believes that problems such as global warming, environmental pollution, resource depletion, ecological degradation, and the loss of biodiversity are much worse than we are able to understand, willing to admit, or tend to estimate.

Fundamental Cause: Not Treating Nature Correctly

The reasons for global environmental deterioration are deep-seated. Though we cannot rule out the influence of reverse ecological succession, the fact remains that the most fundamental cause of global environmental deterioration is humankind's failure to treat nature correctly. Human beings have made irreparable mistakes due to their biased understanding of the relationship between humans and nature. The predatory exploitation of resources and irrational modes of production and lifestyles that came with the Industrial Revolution have had a devastating impact on ecosystems and the environment.

Traditional industrial civilization was undoubtedly a revolutionary step forward from agricultural civilization, creating much higher productivity, huge material wealth, as well as technological and cultural achievements. However, the shortcomings of industrial civilization are not difficult to see: it is extremely profit-driven, greedy, predatory, aggressive, and even crazy in nature, its values and approach to development being the rapid accumulation of wealth and capital at any cost. In recent centuries, under the influence of these ideas, developed industrial countries in the West engaged in an unprecedented campaign to conquer, plunder, and destroy nature. With this came a long succession of colonial wars which not only saw millions die and hundreds of millions become slaves, but also caused the world's ecological environments to suffer on an unprecedented scale. Many of those who plundered the world's natural resources were proponents of anthropocentrism, the view that human beings are the masters of nature and that all other things in the natural world are mankind's possessions, consumables, and servants. Guided by these notions, they robbed, seized and destroyed without restraint, and led extravagant, luxurious, and extremely wasteful lifestyles. In more than 200 years of industrial history, developed countries in the West have consumed around half of the world's non-renewable resources, which took billions of years to form.

Fact has repeatedly warned us that we cannot rely on traditional industrial civilization to correct its own mistakes when it comes to the environment. Traditional industrial civilization has therefore come to a dead end. Despite this, however, certain developing countries have failed to break away from the developmental mode of traditional industrial civilization as they have sought to industrialize. As a result, within the space of just decades, they have encountered the kind of environmental pollution and ecological degradation that took one or two hundred years to emerge in the West. These countries must now meet the challenge of maintaining a balance between economic development and environmental protection.

Since the latter half of the last century, we have come to the profound realization that industrial civilization is unsustainable. Drawing from the lessons of the past, we have proposed the creation of an ecological civilization, which is characterized by sustainable development and harmony between mankind and nature. Ecological civilization provides us with broader prospects for resolving the environmental crisis and maintaining balance between development and the environment. It represents a substantive step forward from industrial civilization, because it not only embodies the strengths of industrial civilization, but is also able to address its weaknesses and failings by applying brand new ideas. The basic features of ecological civilization can be summarized as follows.

First, human beings are a part of nature. The relationship between human beings and other creatures should be one of equality, friendship, and mutual reliance, as opposed to a relationship in which humans are supreme.

Second, since it is nature that has given us life, we should feel gratitude towards nature, repay nature, and treat nature well. We should not forget the debt that we owe to nature, or treat nature and other creatures violently.

Third, humans are entitled to exploit natural resources, but we must take the tolerance of ecosystems and the environment into account when doing so in order to avoid overexploitation.

Fourth, human beings must follow the moral principles of ensuring equity between people, between countries and between generations in resource exploitation. We should refrain from violating the rights and interests of other people, other countries, and future generations.

Fifth, we should advocate conservation, efficiency, and recycling in the utilization of resources so as to maximize efficiency whilst keeping consumption and the impact on nature to a minimum. Sixth, we should view sustainable development as our highest goal, rejecting the overexploitation of resources and short-sighted acts aimed at gaining quick results.

Seventh, the fruits of development must be enjoyed by all members of society and not monopolized by a small minority.

It is essential that we correct the way we treat nature and assume our rightful position in nature. As the wisest of all creatures, we should give full play to our intelligence and capacity for thought by shouldering the responsibility of caring for, protecting, guiding, and strengthening nature, and ensuring that all of nature's creatures are able to live in harmony and develop in a balanced, orderly, and continuous fashion.

China Still Has Serious Problems

It must be noted that while China has made remarkable achievements in socialist modernization during more than 30 years of reform and opening up, it has also encountered serious environmental problems that are undermining its sustainable development. Fact has demonstrated and will continue to demonstrate that we must take Marxism-Leninism, Mao Zedong Thought, and the theories of socialism with Chinese characteristics as our guide, commit to the path of socialism with Chinese characteristics, implement the Scientific Outlook on Development, which puts people first and seeks to promote comprehensive, balanced, and sustainable development, and build a resource-conserving and environmentally friendly society. These are not only the essence for promoting ecological progress and realizing the transformation of human civilization, but also a prerequisite and solid foundation for ensuring the sound and rapid development of economy and society, the balancing of economic development and environmental protection, the establishment of a harmonious society, and the improvement of people's wellbeing.

There are two old Chinese sayings which, through their dialectical materialism, reveal to us the key to success in any undertaking. The first is: to go undefeated in a hundred battles, you must know both the enemy and yourself. The second is: success belongs to those who are prepared, and failure to those who are not. If we are to reverse the trend of environmental degradation and save the biosphere, we must correctly assess the state of our living environment, face up to environmental problems instead of trying to conceal them, use scientific means to anticipate dangers that lurk ahead, and sincerely reflect on our maltreatment of nature. Once we have acknowledged our errors we must take action to correct them. To do this, we must enhance our sense of mission, danger, and responsibility, and take the necessary measures to turn a precarious situation into a favorable one, so as to realize a sound balance between development and the environment.

It is about time that we changed our way of thinking and discarded our concept of a traditional industrial civilization in favor of a modern ecological one. It is about time that we put an end to our irrational modes of development and consumption, and made efforts to save the earth's biosphere.

Facing a Magnificent Struggle

The struggle to save the biosphere and transform our civilization from a traditional industrial civilization to a modern ecological civilization will be an endeavor more magnificent than any seen before in human history, and a complex social undertaking of huge proportions. It will require that we humans carefully consider, correctly understand, and answer a series of questions, some of which are as follows: What is the relationship between human beings and nature? Is it one of the conqueror and the conquered, the dominator and the dominated, and the ruler and the ruled? Or is it one of equality, friendship, harmony, coexistence, and mutual flourishing? Why is earth the only cradle of life among the vast number of celestial bodies in universe? What is the earth's biosphere, and how will ordinal or reversed ecological succession affect the survival and development of human beings? Which biological systems support and maintain the earth's biosphere? Is it inevitable that the survival and development of the human race will come at the expense of ecosystems and the environment? How should we understand the relationship between promoting an ecological civilization and transforming our modes of development and consumption? How should we deal with the contradiction between limited natural resources and limitless human desire? Should we make up for the huge damage caused to nature by long-term overexploitation? If so, how do we repay this debt? Should we let nature rest and regain its strength like humans do when they become old or ill? What is the role of science and technology in saving the biosphere? What is the relationship between population growth and resources, environment and sustainable development? What do the constant wars of human beings mean to nature? How do we give full play to the role of law and ethics as effective means of guaranteeing environmental protection and the salvation of the biosphere? Why must we improve our methods and standards for evaluating economic and social development? How should the countries of the world cooperate and coordinate with one another in saving the earth's biosphere and developing ecological civilization?

Drawing lessons from both our successes and failures in interacting with nature, we must see the global environmental crisis for what it is, and work out the relevant theories, ways of thinking, and counter-measures as we commit ourselves to the path of promoting ecological civilization.

This article originally appeared in Red Flag Manuscript, No.22, 2012. The author is former Vice Chairman of the Standing Committee of the National People's Congress of China. Note: This article is a slightly abridged version of the preface of the book Saving the Earth's Biosphere—Concerning the Transformation of Human Civilization, which was edited by the author and published by Xinhua Press in September 2012.

BOOK REVIEW: Slavery by Another Name, by Douglas A. Blackmon

By Ted Pearson

I recently finished reading this book, subtitled "The Re-Enslavement of Black Americans from the Civil War to World War II." In my opinion, every person who wants to understand the heavy weight of racism on the United States today would do well to read this book.

The profound mistrust of the US criminal justice system among African Americans is rooted in the system of convict labor documented by Blackmon. That system is at the root of the persistent huge and growing chasm between rich and poor and Black and white in the United States. It is at the root of the new wave of mass incarcerations of Black and Latino men and women. Convict slave labor of the post-Civil War South was not only very profitable. It was absolutely indispensable to corporations for breaking any strike that might have been attempted by free workers. Scabs did not have to be recruited. Convict slaves simply replaced strikers. The whip replaced wages.

Film Version Won Award

A PBS documentary based on the book narrated by Lawrence Fishburne won Official Selection of the 2012 Sundance Film Festival. In my opinion, the film's dramatizations fail to convey the horrors of the conditions, torture, disease and death in the slave labor camps of the South documented by Blackmon. To depict the murders, beatings, starvation and conditions under which the "new slaves" of the post Civil War South lived and labored would not have been possible on public television. (The documentary can be viewed at http://www.pbs.org/tpt/slavery-by-another-name/watch/.)

I am not new to the struggle against racism. One could say I was born into it; as a child of 12 I left Louisville, Kentucky with my mother in 1954,

fleeing from the racist repression of the state that had charged and convicted Carl Braden with conspiracy to overthrow the state government by
selling a house in a white suburb to an African American family.

I had heard about the convict leasing system in the South, through which
men and women, overwhelmingly African American, were sentenced to
hard labor. More recently the works of Angela Davis [ii] and Michelle
Alexander [iii] have noted the continuity between the convict leasing
system and the current mass incarceration of African Americans.

I was unprepared, however, for the scope and barbarity of this system
documented by Blackmon. The new slaves numbered in the hundreds
of thousands. They were rented out to work in mines, mills, quarries,
factories, and plantations. Their "contracts" were bought and sold as had
been their forbearers under chattel slavery. Corporate slave enterprises
built the wealth of the "new" southern capitalist class. Many were later
taken over by Wall Street banks and corporations such as US Steel. Their
true history has been erased.

Slaves 'Not Ready' for Democracy

In its place we have the mythology taught in our schools as US history
which covers up this crime. It not only white-washes ante-bellum slavery, suggesting that "only a few" slave owners were cruel. The official
mythology acknowledges that slavery was wrong, but tells us that it was
eliminated at the end of the Civil War. It tells us that the freed slaves
were not equipped for democracy, that they tended toward idleness, lust
and crime and required the kind and gentle hand of white men to help
them improve.

I always understood and rejected this mythology as an attempt to justify
chattel slavery and Jim Crow segregation. However, Blackmon makes
it clear, that this was the rationale for maintaining a slave system long
after it was presumably banished by the 13th Amendment to the US
Constitution in 1865. The convict leasing system re-enslaved tens of
thousands of free men and women who were Black.

Any white person could accuse any Black person of any "crime," including
vagrancy (being alive with no money or proof of a job), gambling, drink-
ing, swearing, being impolite to a white person, and very commonly,
breaking a contract, or failure to pay a debt. A local justice of the peace
would "hold court" and find the victim guilty. A fine would be assessed
plus court costs. A representative of a corporate mine, factory, or plan-
tation would pay the fine plus costs, and the victim would be forced to
make his mark on a contract to work for the enterprise for a set period in
order to pay off the debt. At the end of the contract the prisoner would

often have incurred new debts, fines, or costs. Often the only escape was through death.

The contract would require the purchaser to keep the prisoner locked up, often permanently in chains. There were no requirements for food and clothing, and many starved and died from exposure. No punishment was off-limits. Whippings and beatings were standard punishments for failing to meet production quotas. There were no exceptions for the sick, or those injured by the beatings. Many convict slaves were whipped multiple times in a day. If a beating disabled a convict he was often shot and killed. The owner would simply order more convict slaves from the local sheriff or justice of the peace.

The system established and reinforced a culture in which being Black was to be a criminal. It was transformed into the current system of mass incarceration of African Americans, which has been aptly dubbed the "new Jim Crow" by Michelle Alexander. This system has terrorized African Americans for over 8 generations after slavery purportedly ended, and barred them from almost all paths of upward mobility such as those open to European and other immigrants.

Thousands were literally worked to death in these slave labor camps. Mortality rates as high as 30 per cent were common. Unlike chattel slaves, who had to be bought and were a "capital investment," convict slaves could be "rented" for a few dollars a month. When they died they were easily replaced. The bodies of thousands lie buried in unmarked graves. Many were never recorded as having been charged or convicted of any crime. Many were effectively nameless, lost to their families from whom they were stolen when they disappeared into the maw of the new slavery.

Nazi-like Conditions of the New Slaves

Conditions in the slave labor camps of the factories, mines, mills and fields of the "new" south compare with those in the Nazi slave labor camps during World War II. Unlike Europe's Jews and others targeted by the Nazis, the victims of the new American slavery were usually illiterate and without connections or influence. Their capture and lease as convict slave laborers was often unrecorded. They were often nameless to their masters. Their families lived in such terror that they did not talk about what happened. The new slaves of the United States in the south and their graves just disappeared into the mists of history.

The official mythology is so pervasive that recently Rodney Mims Cook, Jr., a noted architect whose family is descended from James English, one of the leading corporate slavers, campaigned for a monument in down-town Atlanta in tribute to the "great families" that pioneered and built the city after the Civil War, including English, Joel Hurt and others whose fortunes were built through large-scale industrial use of slave labor. The monument has now been completed. The "Millennium Gate Museum" dominates central Atlanta today.

Blackmon, a white native of the South and Wall Street Journal Atlanta Bureau Chief, spent years reconstructing the history of these men and women and the system that enslaved them, combing the scant records that were kept and interviewing surviving family members. He lays out the social and political debt that the United States as a nation owes to the people of African descent who were kept in a state of slavery and racist repression well past 1945, within the memory of many people still living today. Indeed, chain gangs of slave convict laborers did not completely end in the US until 1955, and some states have re-introduced them since 1995, notably Alabama and Arizona.

Blackmon notes that "U. S. Law is unequivocal that the deaths of execu-tives who were responsible for dubious actions don't end a company's legal obligations." Blackmon establishes in chilling detail the social costs of four centuries of racism and slavery. These costs are a debt that must be paid by our society as a whole.

----

[i] Blackmon, Douglas A., Slavery by Another Name, January 2009, Ran-dom House, Inc.
[ii] Davis, Angela, Are Prisons Obsolete? Seven Stories Press, 2003, Davis devotes much of Chapter 2 to this history.
[iii] Alexander, Michelle, The New Jim Crow: Mass Incarceration in the Age of Color Blindness, The New Press, 2010, p. 31. Alexander cites the present work by Blackmon.

Ted Pearson is an organizer with the National Alliance Against Racism and Political Repression in Chicago, as well as a CCDS National Commit-tee member.

FILM: Anne Braden: Southern Patriot

Why You Should See and Use this Important Documentary

By Janet Tucker

"Anne Braden: Southern Patriot is an inspiring tribute to an extraordinary woman and an even more compelling set of ideas: namely, that we all have an important role to play in the struggle for racial and economic justice, and that there is more than one way to live in white skin. Anne was a hero of the first order, modeling white allyship and solidarity across lines of color for over 50 years. That few Americans will have heard her story before now is a sad commentary on the inadequacy of our nation's educational system, and an even more distressing indication of how often bravery and courage are overlooked when they emanate from those who challenge some of our most cherished myths about American democracy. This film is a must-see."
--Tim Wise

Author and Historian, Robin D.G. Kelley, had this to say about the film, Anne Braden: Southern Patriot : "A magnificent portrait of the Anne Braden I knew: courageous, militantly anti-racist to the core. Anne Braden changed my life; this film will change yours." Let her change your life and the lives of those around you.

Everyone should see this important film. What is more important, it should be part of our organizing toolbox. This fine film by filmmakers Anne Lewis and Mimi Pickering tells the life story of Anne Braden, who was born in Louisville, Kentucky but grew up in Anniston, Alabama. Braden points out that is where they burned the Freedom Riders' bus in 1961. In Louisville as a young adult Braden embarked on a life dedicated to the fight for social justice. She was not deterred by threats of violence and jail which is what happened when she and her husband, Carl, bought a house for a black couple in an all white neighborhood in 1954. Initially the house was shot at and a cross was burned in the front yard; finally the house was bombed. Rather than going after the whites who had planted the bomb, Anne and Carl and five other whites were charged with sedition, for creating tension between the races and in that way attempting to overthrow the government of Kentucky.

The Braden house was raided, socialist and communist books were found (as well as Turgenev and Dostoevsky) and the trial became a trial against books. Carl was sentenced to 15 years, a sentence which was later over-turned on the technicality that you can't commit sedation against a state-it's a federal crime. Anne and Carl Braden kept their commitments to racial justice and first amendments rights. They were part of the mass civil rights movement. Dorothy Zellner of SNCC called Anne Braden "the conscience of civil liberties for the movement." Anne pointed out to white people that this is "not something we're called on to help people of color with. We need to become involved with it as if our lives depended on it because, in truth, they do." She was clear that in everything we took up, the struggle against racism needed to be at the core.

Centrality of Racism

We cannot win economic justice or any struggle without addressing the racism that is used to divide us. A staunch fighter for economic and racial justice her whole life, Anne is a living example of the intersection of class, race and gender. In this film, Anne states that society builds prisons around people. She says she was born privileged in a class soci-ety and white in a racist society. She said she had to break out of those prisons. "The hardest thing was class. I don't know that I could have ever broken out of what I call the race prison if I hadn't dealt with class. It's that assumption that is so embedded in you that you don't realize it's there - that your crowd is supposed to be running things."

Anne pointed out that as long as race could be used to get a majority of white Americans to oppose efforts for a more just society, there will be no hope of ending poverty, homelessness, environmental destruction, inequality, or of making the kind of transformative change imperative if democracy is to be real in our nation. She showed us that not just de-mocracy, but our very humanity is tied to refusing to be silent in the face of the devastating reality of racism in the lives of people of color." (Cate Fosl and Carla Wallace, op-ed in Louisville Courier Journal)

Anne and Carl worked for many years for SCEF, the Southern Conference Educational Fund, an organization that worked across the south for ra-cial and economic justice. SCEF stood strong against racist attacks and red baiting. Anne was the editor of their newspaper, The Southern Pa-triot In 1980 Anne spoke to a large rally made up of people from across the south who gathered to protest the murder of 5 members of the Communist Workers Party in Greensboro, NC by the Klan, "The real danger comes from people in high places, from the halls of Congress to the boardrooms of our big corporations, who tell white people that if their paychecks are eaten up by taxes it's not because of our bloated military budget but because of government programs that benefit black people. If young whites are unemployed, it's because blacks are getting all the jobs. Our problem is the people in power who are creating a scapegoat mentality. That's what is creating the danger of a fascist movement in America."

Anne was reluctant to have this film made. She told a class at the University of Louisville, "They're doing this documentary on me which embarrasses me highly, but really what they're trying to do is look at the movements I've been a part of through the lens of my life." And this is exactly what the film does. Anne was very much a teacher but much of her teaching was done on the picket line, at a demonstration or while stuffing envelopes.

Bob Zellner said of her, "Anne had taught us you could be for an open political discussion... you can be for integration... and you could still be a good person... a normal person. If it was Rosa Parks and Martin Luther King who convinced me to join the struggle, it was Anne Braden who showed me how to do it."

'White Supremacy' Is the More Accurate Term

Anne spoke to the Midwest Regional meeting of CCDS in March of 2004. She emphasized learning from history. "This country was built on white supremacy - I prefer the term 'white supremacy' to 'racism' - because its more what we really mean - you don't have to get into endless arguments about whether Blacks can be racist. So, the country was built on white supremacy and if you understand it that way - it is not just a wart on the body politic - this is where the original wealth of this country came from - from slavery and the slave trade. It was built into the institutions - the courts and everything from the beginning - so when anytime in history the African Americans organize and move, it shakes everything." She talked about how the civil rights movement shook the very foundation of the South and broke the police state that existed there.

Anne was more than anything else, an organizer "Those of us who want to create a new world - or just stop a police state or whatever is coming out of Washington - we have to organize the unorganized. We can't just be what I think passes for organizing among people on the left but other places too, which I call 'reshuffling the organized'. We tend to get together with people who already agree with us and we may talk about some plans but it's comfortable to be with people we agree with.

We have to do that to keep our own strength up - we give each other strength. But we have got to go out and talk to these people that are not in our movement!"

Anne believed in organizing people and in the ability of people to change. She did not think that guilt was a productive emotion and says in the film that most white people she saw that got involved in the struggle did so because they envisioned a different kind of world, one that they wanted to be a part of. "The meaning of life is in that struggle which human beings have always been able to do - to envision something better... that's what makes human beings divine." Hearing Martin Luther King, Jr. portrayed as a "dreamer," she instead insisted that "Martin Luther King was not a dreamer, he was a revolutionary,." and she would quote from MLK's Riverside Church speech: "True compassion is more than flinging coins to a beggar... true compassion realizes that a society that produces beggars needs to be entirely restructured."

The filmmakers, Anne Lewis and Mimi Pickering, have done us a great service. This highly powerful and enjoyable film should be widely used. This is a wonderful film just to see but it is a powerful film seen with others. Let us learn from history through Anne's eyes and life. Let us use this to organize the unorganized by taking this film into our communities.

The film can be ordered from Appalshop.org, http://www.annebraden-film.org/ and California Newsreel http://www.newsreel.org/nav/title.asp?tc=CN0236

CCDS Convention 2013: Draft Main Resolution

This document is a draft of the main resolution on the 2013 convention agenda. CCDS conventions follow democratic process in discussion, amendment and voting on this and all resolutions. Your active participation in thorough discussion of this document before the convention is a crucial part of the democratic process. Please post your comments at http://www.ccds-discussion.org/?p=2337.

TURNING POINT: Growing Dangers and Growing Progressive Strength Require a Bolder Strategy

In an 1859 study of conflict and social transformation, Karl Marx wrote,

> *"It is always necessary to distinguish between the material transformation of the economic conditions of production, which can be determined with the precision of natural science, and the legal, political, religious, artistic or philosophic-in short, the ideological forms in which men become conscious of this conflict and fight it out."*

Let this guide our pre-convention discussion.

Economic Conditions

Three decades ago, the post-WW2 economic boom began to stagnate in the United States, Europe and Japan. At first uneven, a global pattern became dominant. To shore up declining rates of profit, the bourgeoisie dismantled economic regulatory mechanisms. Employing new technologies, they moved production to countries on the low-wage periphery of capitalism. At home, wages, and then consumption, stagnated. Economic expansion relied increasingly on loans and other financial instruments. This secured the dominance of financiers in the economy and the state.

Austerity. After looting public treasuries in a series of regressive tax cuts, and still more looting to recoup staggering investment losses, financiers now demand cuts in social programs. These programs, the social wage, support the standard of living of the working class. The cuts are called "austerity" - for whom?

Financiers spoke in a Spring, 2012 Forbes editorial:

> "If these governments can quickly balance their budgets and lower the level of nominal debt outstanding; it gives them a chance to restore investors' confidence in the bond market ... and offers the hope that the private sector can rapidly supplant the erstwhile reliance on public sector spending."

Their jargon disguises their intent. The financial bourgeoisie is not against public spending - on the military. Their real goal is to reduce total wages by gradually eliminating the social wage. The more wages fall, the greater their take. Thus they undermine the part of the state that provides what their pundits deride as "entitlements." Yes, medical care in old age and in poverty, food stamps to alleviate starvation, and free and compulsory public education are entitlements, human rights for which we will fight.

War. Requiring OPEC to trade oil in US dollars has underwritten the international dominance of US financial institutions since 1973. OPEC member states Iraq, Iran, Libya and Venezuela began to resist in 2000. Rather than recognize their sovereignty, the US government decided to maintain the petrodollar system by perpetuating a state of war in the oil-rich regions. Facing an expanding arsenal - guns, bombs, corporate mercenaries, devastating blockades cloaked in diplomacy, missiles launched from remote-control drones - the peoples of those regions pay with their lives, as do the people of the United States

The emergence of China as a world economic power, as a competitor for natural resources and markets, and as a creditor to the capitalist states has been met with the establishment of a second US military focus: the South China Sea. By militarily supporting Taiwan separatists, Japanese revanchists and the South Korean right, US policy creates international tensions aimed at weakening China and hindering peaceful economic and social cooperation in Asia.

Climate Danger. In 2009, the U.S. National Academy of Science joined the national academies of a dozen other countries to report:

> "Climate change is happening even faster than previously estimated; global CO2 emissions since 2000 have been higher than even the highest predictions, Arctic sea ice has been melting at rates much faster than predicted, and the rise in the sea level has become more rapid.

Feedbacks in the climate system might lead to much more rapid climate changes. The need for urgent action to address climate change is now indisputable. For example, limiting global warming to 2°C would require a very rapid worldwide implementation of all currently available low carbon technologies."

The world's scientists have unequivocally concluded that the need for "very rapid" action is "urgent."

Why do the world's governments take no action? London's Carbon Tracker Initiative estimates that the world's proven oil, gas and coal reserves contain the equivalent of 2,795 gigatons of CO2. Scientists estimate that limiting global warming to 2°C requires limiting CO2 release to less than 565 gigatons. However, as Bill McKibben writes in the Rolling Stone of August 2, 2012:

"John Fullerton, a former managing director at JP Morgan who now runs the Capital Institute, calculates that at today's market value, those 2,795 gigatons of carbon emissions are worth about $27 trillion. Which is to say, if you paid attention to the scientists and kept 80 percent of it underground, you'd be writing off $20 trillion in assets. The numbers aren't exact, of course, but that carbon bubble makes the housing bubble look small by comparison. It won't necessarily burst-we might well burn all that carbon, in which case investors will do fine. But if we do, the planet will crater."

The financial capitalists stand in the way of a rational solution to civilization's crisis of existence- climate change.

Drawing Conclusions

Marx continued the 1859 passage cited above observing that new conditions mature within the old society, and concluded:

"Humankind thus inevitably sets itself only such tasks as it is able to solve, since closer examination will always show that the problem itself arises only when the material conditions for its solution are already present or at least in the course of formation."

The 99% must empower itself; that is where the solutions lie.

Politics

Federal Elections. In 2010, Tea Party demagoguery and lackluster Democratic leadership lured crisis-shocked workers into handing Republicans substantial gains in Congress and in state legislatures. In 2012, the

Progressive Majority behind President Obama's 2008 victory prevailed against a Republican campaign of racism, misogyny, homophobia and rejection of science. While ruling class elements paid the obscene media bill, the election was won with a powerful grassroots campaign by trade unionists, Blacks, Latinos, women, gays, seniors and youth—a social bloc based in the working class.

State Elections. In 2012, the two parties' fortunes in state elections ran counter to those at the federal level. New districts followed Republican maps, the fallout of the 2010 elections. Thirty-eight one-party state legislatures emerged in 2012 - twenty-four Republican, including all Southern states but Kentucky. Yet again, crisis-shocked workers - especially in impoverished Southern states with little union organization - fell for messages of hate from the network of institutions designed to maintain capitalist power. Indeed, politics is much more than elections.

Politics is the struggle for hearts and minds; it is the struggle for class power. People generally see politics as annual public contests at the ballot box, the outcomes of which are thought to rest on a public discussion of the candidates' personal characters and general ideals. Yet the function of this image, like the curtain in the Wizard of Oz, is only to conceal the real sources and mechanisms of power. The political power of the ruling class rests ultimately on its ownership of the main strategic economic assets, including key media outlets. Because it wishes to stifle the exercise of power by the working class, the ruling class seeks to limit working class understanding of how power works.

Yes, elections are political, as is the whole realm of the state, which encompasses powers of coercion such as the new Jim Crow of mass incarceration, as well as public policy and the rest of the public sector, from sanitation services to social security. The struggle for democracy occurs not only in voting booths, but also in workplaces and communities. In fact, the Voting Rights Act was not won by voting. It was won in pitched battles in civil society, the political arena outside the family, the state and the economy, which we sometimes call the streets.

Wikileaks' use of the internet to open the US government's cloak of secrecy is politics in the field of the commons, the intellectual and natural resources that belong by right to all society. Transforming elements of the commons into private property is called privatization or enclosure. The historic defense of the commons against enclosure has come down to saving the fresh water supply from privatization, and to protecting crops and human genes from corporate ownership by patent. The outcome of this struggle is of fundamental significance to democracy: will private corporate interests control access to water, food and medicine? Classes are based in economic relations which makes the economy the fundamental arena of politics. Trade union organizing and campaigns for equal pay for equal work are politics in the field of the economy. Workers' cooperatives benefit worker-participants and model an economic alternative to capitalism. Especially in light of the danger posed by carbon emissions, the highest political question in the field of the economy is what society produces and how.

Politics runs through all these channels, day after day, year after year, and it is impossible to develop a class political strategy without recognizing that fact.

Alliances. The Communist Manifesto informs us: "The proletarian movement is the self-conscious, independent movement of the immense majority, in the interest of the immense majority," it encourages strategic alliances, and advises us: "The Communists fight for the attainment of the immediate aims, for the enforcement of the momentary interests of the working class; but in the movement of the present, they also represent and take care of the future of that movement." As the present multi-class electoral alignment strains under austerity, war and climate danger, we must weave together a mass formation independent of the capitalist plutocracy.

New Alignments, New Strategies

Retreating under capitalist onslaught, union membership in the United States, the European Union and Japan continued its downward spiral. Fighting defensive battles, the Left has also retreated. Yet spontaneous militant movements - the Arab Spring, the Indignados of Spain, the workers' occupations of the statehouses in Wisconsin, Indiana and Ohio, Occupy Wall Street -rose up and shook society by the shoulders. The 99% had no more space to retreat - the banks had foreclosed our homes! Business-as-usual was shattered, political discourse was changed from the need to cut social services to the need to end gross disparities in income and wealth. We were revived.

A new consciousness of the struggle for democracy emerged in the protests against the "stand your ground" vigilante laws and the killing of Trayvon Martin, in the protests against the death penalty and the judicial murder of Troy Davis, and in the struggles of courageous undocumented workers and students who openly rode the UndocuBus and fought for the Dream Act. New forms of labor organizing appeared and spread, drawing working class communities into direct action at the workplace: the long campaign at Republic Windows and Doors that gave birth to a workers' coop in Chicagoland, the Chicago teachers' strike, the nationwide actions at Wal-Mart, and the growing Southern Workers' Assembly.

Struggles involving communities in direct action to organize the work-place - with or without a sanctioned election - project beyond the current state of the trade unions toward a growing working class movement. It is a rejection of business unionism, which reduced unions to fee-for-service organizations on behalf of the narrowest workplace interests - the Cold War mold into which unions were forced, as socialists and communists were kicked out of elected leadership and staff positions. The European general strikes against austerity, of similar significance, united the labor movement, calling upon, and serving, the whole class.

Emerging is a democracy movement based in the working class, one capable of winning demands from the capitalist system by following the bold path of the Civil Rights Movement in an earlier day. The Left must recover its revolutionary heritage, help this movement forward, and, along with our allies in labor, draw the difficult lessons on the need to overcome Cold War remnants and other deterrents to independent initiative.

The Rainbow Model. Looking forward, formations such as North Caro-lina's Historic Thousands on Jones Street Coalition, South Carolina's Pro-gressive Network and Ties That Bind Coalition, and Kentuckians for the Commonwealth, could play a special role in state-level political strug-gles, linking the economy, civil society and electoral politics. From the viewpoint of electoral politics - by walking picket lines and taking up street-level struggles that matter to our communities - this link means constituency building. From the viewpoint of civil society, this link can drive accountability of elected officials.

During the 1980s, the Rainbow Coalition played this role at the national level. After President Carter fired UN Ambassador Andrew Young for meeting with Palestinian representatives, Reverend Jackson's dramatic 1979 mission to Palestine garnered support in the African-American community. In 1984, he negotiated the return from Syria of a captured US pilot, boosting his presidential campaign. The Rainbow became a phenomenon in 1988, when Jackson walked the picket line with striking paper workers in Jay, Maine and supported family farmers in Greenville, Iowa. The Rainbow linked to mutual- advantage movements in the econ-omy, civil society and the state.

Some Rainbow adherents envisioned it as a lobby to pressure Demo-crats. However, in a 1985 paper, Rainbow Coalition International Direc-tor Jack O'Dell took a different view:

"The Rainbow Coalition is a mass political movement, committed to the expansion of the definition and practice of democracy in our coun-try, including the realization of economic justice. As such it has to be bold enough to perceive of itself as the historic replacement for the existing two-party system: one prepared to act as a 'dual authority,' carrying out political education, developing the public's insights into the systemic character of many of the nation's problems, and consequently proposing solutions to these problems that are germane."

Alliance Anatomy. The Rainbow campaigns contributed to President Obama's electoral successes. But why did Obama's presidential bid succeed while Jackson's failed? The Obama campaign was based on a far larger alignment, a multi-class alignment that encompassed class interests from the working class suffering from economic stagnation, to Wall Street bankers expecting a titanic federal bailout. Clearly, the politics of such an alignment is unreliable for workers, but acceptable to the ruling elite. The class basis of the Rainbow, on the other hand, lay with family farmers and workers. Its political program was anathema to the ruling class, and was not destined to capture the presidency in the 1980s. But the future belongs to the Rainbow.

These two formations have historical names. The Popular Front was the multi-class alignment that emerged in the United States, as well as in other countries, during WWII and the anti-fascist struggle. Within it, the deep alliance around the militant CIO unions and the CIO Political Action Committee was termed the United Front. Similar formations emerged in other countries as well. With President Franklin Roosevelt's death, the Popular Front suffered a serious blow, as bourgeois participants turned against their working class partners, a prelude to Cold War. While the united front could continue, it organized a wave of strikes for Roosevelt's second bill of rights. Its last recognizable mass effort was the 1948 Progressive Party presidential campaign of Henry Wallace, although it was officially opposed by the CIO. In general, relations among parties to a popular front will be strained on precisely those issues where the interests of the united front diverge from those of leading capitalists.

Over the last several years, a multi-class popular front – what CCDS terms the Progressive Majority – came together to support the presidential campaigns of Barack Obama and to defend against the political right wing. The United Front - from the state-level formations to the One Nation Working Together coalition mentioned above - is what can change the Progressive Majority from a defensive alignment to a transformative alignment. The Progressive Majority is a framework in which social leadership can be contested by the United Front while it acts to shift the terrain of struggle in its favor and to isolate the financial bourgeoisie.

Transition. The transition in the Progressive Majority from leadership by sectors of the capitalist class to leadership by the working class forces of the United Front may be extended-punctuated perhaps by acute economic, military or climate crises. This transition requires a more self-conscious working class, which in turn requires a more unified and larger Left. The Left must help to forward the emerging united fronts by building up a body of capable activists at the grass roots. Of course, we seek to retain what is useful in the Progressive Majority. A sound chess strategy looks, not just at the next move, but at the next three.

The Left

Though we struggle with organizational fragmentation and lingering feelings of political isolation, the Left has an indispensable role to play in supporting emerging strategic formations and encouraging their independence of action. Together with allies, our central task is organization-building. The Left's distinct contribution in that central task is revolutionary education. In educating new activists, we are uniquely able to impart the sensitivity necessary for service to the class at its grass roots, as well as the broad understanding of social dynamics necessary for visionary leadership. The Left must work, tactfully and unrelentingly, to rebuff neo-liberal influences and to nourish class, political, cultural and moral solidarity and democracy.

For some years, Left organizations have cooperated in popular struggles. This cooperation could be deepened qualitatively by developing a common southern strategy. Organizing gains in the South - historic base of the Black masses, locus of new manufacturing investments - have a multiplier effect throughout the country. This could broaden the foundation for organizational unity. The CCDS focus on the intersection of class, race and gender contributes to lasting unity among allies.

In poll after poll, a significant number of youth favor socialism over capitalism. We socialists take heart, and proceed with determination for our common future. CCDS calls on its allies and members to convene in Pittsburgh in July, 2013 to assess the concrete situation and the quality of our work since the last convention, and to orient ourselves to the future. There will be an expanded opportunity to plan our work in strategic areas of struggle.

The Lost Writings of SDS...A New Collection Edited by Carl Davidson

Revolutionary Youth & the New Working Class

The Praxis Papers, the Port Authority Statement, the RYM Documents and Other Lost Writings of SDS

Edited by Carl Davidson

This is a fascinating new collection of 12 essays and documents from the New Left of the late 1960s, gathered and commented on by Carl Davidson, a national leader of SDS at the time.

'Revolutionary Youth and the New Working Class' contains key sources illuminating a critical transition period in the American left, as well as a number of ideas still relevant.

Most important is the 'Port Authority Statement', actually titled 'Toward a Theory of Social Change, and written by Robert Gottlieb, Gerry Tenney and David Gilbert. Passed around in mimeographed form, only about a third of it was ever put into print in SDS's newspaper, until factional struggles set it aside. Met to replace the Port Huron Statement, it is remarkable for many insights still holding up today.

The collection includes other 'Praxis Papers,' including three by Davidson, the Revolutionary Youth Movement documents that replied to the Weatherman faction, and the original 'White Blindspot' documents. About half the content has been scattered across the internet, but much of it has been newly digitized and now available in both e-book and paperback form from Changemaker Publications. Go to the site for the full contents, and contact the editor at carld717@gmail.com for bulk rates.

To see the full contents go to http://www.lulu.com/product/paperback/revolutionary-youth-and-the-new-working-class/17144702 and click 'preview' under the picture of the cover

The 'Lone Ranger' Period Is Over!
We Need You to Join Us....

We're inviting you to join the Committees of Correspondence for Democracy and Socialism. We need you help in building a progressive majority for peace, justice and equally—and then pushing on to a new society where these will be the rule, rather than the exception. Socialism is being more widely discussed today than any time since the 1960s, and you can't take part in it fully without a socialist organization.

Working with many others, CCDS aims to end existing wars and prevent new ones. We oppose the current austerity being imposed upon the working people, a burden made even heavier by militarism and the hidden costs of non-renewable energy systems. We need a global order based on peaceful relations among nations, mutual respect and human rights, and the creation of economies that can exist in harmony with nature.

You can make a difference. Lend a hand in organizing with others to fight for a progressive agenda in the streets, workplaces, communities of faith and schools. It's not crowded up front, so sign up today!

Fill out and mail today.*
  Yes, I'd like to join the CCDS. Enclosed is my check for:
  $ _____.
  I'd like a subscription to Dialogue & Initiative. Enclosed is my check for $12.50 (Non-Members, $15.00).
  I know good causes need money. Here is my contribution of
  $_____.

Name _____
Address _____
City _____ State _____ Zip _____
Phone_____ Email _____

Make check payable to Committees of Correspondence, and mail to: Committees of Correspondence, P.O. Box 437, New York, NY 10018-0008, Phone (212) 868-3733

Email: national@cc-ds.org Web: www.cc-ds.org

* The Committees of Correspondence for Democracy and Socialism (CCDS) is a national organization dedicated to the struggle for justice, equality, democracy, peace and socialism. The annual membership is $36 for individuals; $18 for unemployed, seniors, youth, and others with low income; $48 for households

www.ingramcontent.com/pod-product-compliance
Lightning Source LLC
Chambersburg PA
CBHW022001170526
45157CB00003B/1086